HOW TO GET THE MOST OUT OF
Trade Shows

Steve Miller

Foreword by William W. Mee

NTC Business Books
a division of *NTC Publishing Group* • Lincolnwood, Illinois USA

1991 Printing

Published by NTC Business Books, a division of NTC Publishing Group,
4255 West Touhy Avenue, Lincolnwood (Chicago), Illinois 60646-1975 U.S.A.
Manufactured in the United States of America.
Library of Congress Catalog Card Number: 90-60184

1 2 3 4 5 6 7 8 9 BC 9 8 7 6 5 4 3 2

To Kay—My best friend, my partner, and my love.
I promised you it would never be dull.

CONTENTS

Foreword

Experienced exhibitors and attendees know that there is far more to trade show success than "just being there." There are many "old hands" still working the circuit who remember when trade show participants were more concerned with having a good time than they were with recognizing the opportunity for focused marketing and a chance to learn more about their business.

Trade show marketing has changed noticeably in the last twenty-five years as a result of the rising cost of business-to-business selling, the remarkable increase in the number of expositions being held, and the expansion of exhibition facilities, which has led to a new appreciation of the medium as an effective marketing tool.

Participation in trade shows appears easy. Exhibitors sign up for space, set up their booths, and hope for the selling "frenzy" to begin. Although minor selling miracles are still possible, waiting for them to occur is trying and uncertain. However the results speak for themselves: 40 percent of all first-time exhibitors do not sign up for a second go-round. As is the case with other high-reward business opportunities, "knowing the territory" and using that knowledge to one's advantage make all the difference.

Steve Miller, an independent trade show marketing consultant with eleven years of international trade show experience to his credit, has really covered the territory. In *How to Get the Most out of Trade Shows* he offers the reader a guided tour over this very complex terrain. It would not be unusual for exhibitors to double or even triple their production of qualified leads for the same show over the next two years by following the well-thought-out plans that Miller outlines in this outstanding book.

Miller's engaging and informative approach, which stresses preparation and *execution*, provides easily understood solutions to the most perplexing trade show problems. The trade show industry heartily welcomes *How to Get the Most out of Trade Shows*.

William W. Mee
President, Trade Show Bureau

Preface

Several years ago, as a rookie salesperson in my twenties, I was required by my company to work at a number of trade shows each year. They were always a source of mixed emotions for me. Although I was excited to discover all the new products being introduced, I was terrified by the prospect of being accosted by thousands of strangers on the show floor. And while it was fun to make new friends with other exhibitors and dine at fine restaurants every night, the selling success of the trade shows was always poor. Often, there was no selling success. Sometimes I would get a lot of business cards, but, in the long run, very few results.

Then one day, while walking through a major show, I observed that the great majority of exhibits were staffed by people who were sitting down, reading, eating, and generally ignoring attendees. Many booths were not staffed at all! I realized that these companies had no desire to sell! I knew I was on to something.

I began to study trade shows in-depth. I talked with buyers. I watched successful trade show marketers and learned from them. Gradually, I learned how to sell successfully at trade shows. As I climbed the ladder from territorial sales rep to regional sales manager, national sales manager, and eventually vice-president of International Sales and Marketing, I used trade shows as the main thrust of my marketing efforts. Nevertheless, there was a void in my learning. While there were thousands of books on sales, marketing, direct mail, and telemarketing, there were only a handful of books available on trade show marketing. I was forced to learn solely from experience.

After I had been in business as a marketing consultant for some time, clients began asking where they could learn more about trade show marketing. I realized I was in the position to write a strongly needed book, but like most would-be authors, I procrastinated. It wasn't until a fateful dinner with my friends Jim and Henriette Klauser (a successful author in her own right) that I firmly decided to write this book. Thank you both, Jim and Henriette.

I would also like to thank those people who provided their valuable insight, support, and time in helping make this book possible: Bill Mee, Betsy Rogers, Gary Kerr, Jerry Peterson, Phil Wexler, Jim Cathcart, George Walther, Michael Treadwell, Bill Beeh, K. C. Aly, Melinda Lilley, and Larry Steiner. A very special note of thanks belongs to Herb Cartmell and Lynda Wilson of American Image Displays for their input into show planning and booth design. And last, but certainly not least, my heartfelt thanks to Vanna Novak, Randi Freidig, and Marilyn Schoeman Dow; as the other three members of the Speakers4, they have been my biggest boosters and ego-builders during this labor of love.

Introduction: What to Expect from This Book

A trade show can be the best marketing tool you ever use. Trade shows are not cheap, however. Every year, all across the United States and around the world, companies throw away thousands and even millions of dollars on trade shows. An improperly planned exhibit can cause more harm than good.

If you are a new exhibitor or a veteran of hundreds of shows, it's important to understand that a well-run trade show is an investment in the future. And just like any well-managed investment, it provides a return based on initial objectives. This book will give you information on how to plan properly for that investment.

The first-time exhibitor will learn how to select the right trade shows, how to plan ahead, how to design a booth, how to attract prospects to the booth, how to sell on the floor, and how to follow up. It will give you solid information on how to assimilate successful trade shows into your current marketing mix.

For the veteran, this book provides a refresher course on the basics and covers some ideas and techniques that he or she might not know about. Although other trade show books concentrate on the exhibit planning area, this book focuses on the bottom line: active show promotion, training, prospecting, qualifying, floor selling, postshow follow-up, and evaluation.

Forms and checklists are included for all phases of trade show planning and implementation. Much of the information has been compiled through interviews with some of the top trade show marketers in various industries throughout the United States, as well as through discussions with top buyers. This book candidly gives you their impressions about trade shows, including the turnoffs and mistakes made by exhibitors. It'll show you how to attract top buyers to your booth and teach you *how to sell to them.*

This book is easy reading, but is not meant to be skimmed and put away. It's meant to be a workbook. Take notes. Underline. Scribble in the margins. Tear out pages on specific information if you like. But, most of all, select the few things you can use and then act on them. This book is chock full of nuts-and-bolts information that anybody involved with trade shows can use.

Don't put this book on the shelf; it won't do you any good there. Keep it handy and refer to it regularly. Planning for a trade show shouldn't be an afterthought. It takes a total commitment and a thorough knowledge of everything involved. This book will help you get that knowledge and use it.

CHAPTER 1

The Scope of Trade Show Marketing

Imagine this: You're the head buyer for a very large chain of consumer electronics stores, and your secretary buzzes you on the intercom. "Mr. Smith, there's a couple of salespeople from Widget Manufacturing here to see you." You're busy but ask her to show them in anyway.

As they enter, you notice they've brought a magician and two *Playboy* bunnies with them. The bunnies huddle around you, pose for a picture taken by one of the salesmen, stick a little fuzzy bird on the shoulder of your new Giorgio Armani suit, and hand you a plastic bag full of literature. The magician then begins his act—a rapid-fire set of card tricks accompanied by a running monologue telling you how the new Widget will put magic into your sales. Meanwhile, the two salesmen have found a couch in the corner of your office and have lit a couple of very smelly cigars. The magician continues his act while the bunnies preen, smile, and sign scantily clad pictures of themselves for you to take home to your wife. Finally, the magician finishes his act.

One of the salesmen gets up, puts his arm around your shoulders, and, while confidently using his cigar as a pointer, gives you a pitch a used-car salesperson would be proud of. The other salesman grabs your phone and ignores you. During the pitch, the first guy tries to demonstrate the new Widget, but for some reason it won't work. He doesn't break stride. "It's a prototype," he explains, "but trust me, it's the best darn Widget ever made."

When you ask a question, the first salesman goes blank and looks to the second salesman who merely shrugs his shoulders. "Gee, this is such a new product, we'll have to call back to the

1

home office to check on that," they chime. But they ask for your order anyway.

Sound familiar? Well, it may be a little farfetched, but there is a point to all of this. If you wouldn't put up with this type of behavior as a buyer, why on earth would you consider it appropriate as a seller? Why is it that so many companies feel it's necessary to use this approach when marketing at trade shows?

Companies that use such Hollywood tactics to attract trade show buyers are missing the real purpose of the trade show medium. Granted, there is a big difference between making a field sales call and exhibiting your product to thousands of potential customers. But a trade show is a selling medium. Understanding the essential value of trade shows as a low-cost way of reaching new prospects, and knowing what financial effect they can have on your company's future, is imperative.

A Bit of History

Trade shows are big business. According to William Mee, president of the Trade Show Bureau, American industry invests more than $20 billion a year in trade shows to reach more than forty million attendees. In the United States alone, there are more than 10,000 regional, national, and international exhibitions with more than 50,000 companies participating. Of these, the top 2,733 shows attract an average of more than 15,000 attendees.[1] More money is spent on trade shows than on magazine, radio, and outdoor advertising. Only newspapers and television receive substantially greater advertising funds.

Today's megaextravaganza shows vary greatly from the bazaars of biblical times, which were originally set up where caravan routes crossed. For centuries, the bazaar was the central focus for bartering and selling goods, services, information, even people.

[1]This information was taken from conversations with William Mee, president of the Trade Show Bureau, an industry-supported research and educational organization funded by major exhibit industry associations and corporate contributions. The figures from the 2,733 shows specifically came from the 1986 *Tradeshow Week Data Book,* published by Tradeshow Week of Los Angeles, California.

The first real trade show was the 1851 World's Fair in London. Held for seven months in the temporary Crystal Palace, the fair showcased the achievements of the British Empire, then at its peak. The purpose of the World's Fair was to stimulate business for British companies in the international market. (Across the Atlantic in America, trade shows didn't really come into vogue until mass production was developed.)

Modern exhibitions, instead of focusing on general merchandise, have become specialized. If there's an industry or market for a product, it probably has a trade show. Health care, video software, consumer electronics, advertising specialties, toys, and automobiles are examples of industries that sponsor specialized trade shows.

As trade shows proliferate, so have the number of companies exhibiting and attendees registering. The exhibit arena has become tremendously competitive. *Or has it?* Although any good-size show certainly features many innovative displays and clever exhibiting strategies, a closer look reveals disappointing exhibitor behavior: backs turned while prospects examine products on display, eating and smoking while on duty, nonstop chatter with the pretty model as potential prospects stroll by, and ignoring customers while talking on the phone, to name but a few faults.

Also in evidence are the few exhibitors who take the show seriously. They know their products, warmly welcome prospects into their booths, aggressively qualify buyers, and appear alert to opportunity. These exhibitors have profitable shows.

Sponsoring a successful exhibit is a simple process. It's not an easy process, just simple. Understanding the value of a trade show and recognizing its importance in your marketing plan will go a long way toward ensuring your success.

Why Trade Shows Are So Popular

Trade Shows Are Cost Effective

The value of trade shows can be seen through simple mathematics. One survey revealed that the average industrial sales call costs $229.70. It also revealed that an average of 5.5 office calls were required to close, bringing the total cost per sale to

$1,263.35.[2] Compare this to a Trade Show Bureau's Report that found an average per contact cost of $106.70 at trade shows with only .8 follow-up field calls required to close the sale; hence, an average cost per sale of $290.46.[3] In other words, for every one field-generated sale, you could make four exhibit-generated sales! That's cost-effective.

Exposure to New Customers

We all know that salespeople are comfortable calling on old friends—buyers they've been working with for years. They also like to believe that they know their territory better than anyone else. Maybe that's true. But do they know *every* potential customer? Do they really know *every* buyer at *every* company? It's doubtful. There are always new opportunities. The difficulty in making new contacts lies with a basic human condition. Everyone wants to be liked. And cold calling is tough on the ego. It's not fun; it's filled with rejection and is often demoralizing. It involves going to unfamiliar territory and calling strangers for appointments. And that's difficult. Getting to the right person is sometimes like picking your way through a fun house filled with deadends and deception. It is no wonder people don't like to venture outside their comfort zone.

Unfortunately, corporate growth requires new customers. Fortunately, trade shows represent one of the best and most cost-effective ways to obtain them. One of the beauties of trade shows is that buyers come to you. They schedule several days of their own time to travel to a show. They are off their turf. Buyers are there to look for new products for their own businesses. Believe it or not, if you have a product that fills a customer's needs, he or she wants to meet you. In fact, at most established national shows, there are thousands of new prospects waiting to meet you.

According to a Trade Show Bureau "Report," at regional shows, fully 92 percent of the average exhibitor's visitors had not been called on by a salesperson during the previous year. At national shows, a staggering 84 percent of the average exhibitor's

---

[2] McGraw-Hill Lab of Advertising Performance (1985). Specific source is the "Trade Show Bureau Research Report No. 2020," July 1986.
[3] "Trade Show Bureau Research Report No. 2020," July 1986.

contacts had not been called on by the company in over a year.[4] So, if you see 200 legitimate buyers at a national show, 168 of them will be new contacts. How long would it take your sales force to come up with 168 legitimate new prospects?

Three-Dimensional Selling

If there's one advantage that trade shows have over newspapers, magazines, radio, outdoor billboards, television, and even field sales, it's this: At a trade show you can set up your actual product to be displayed in its best light. Selling heavy equipment? Your prospect can climb all over that earthmover of yours and see live demonstrations of just how good it really is. Producing popcorn? A magazine ad doesn't compare to the actual aroma and taste of fresh-popped corn.

Comparison Shopping for Immediate Decisions

Gone shopping for shoes lately? Did you see a pair advertised in the paper and call the store to order them? Or did you just buy the first pair in the first store you stopped at? Of course not. If you're an average shopper, you went down to the local mall. You tried on a few pairs at Steve's Shoes, then went to Shoes R Us to check out their selection. Then you strolled over to Shoe City and finally went to the If the Shoe Fits store. You compared styles, colors, and prices before you made your decision; and you were able to do it all in one convenient location—the mall.

That same advantage exists in trade shows; they resemble a temporary shopping mall. The presence of competitors encourages the buying process. Let's assume a prospect's interest is aroused by a particular type of product. If the interest is generated by a magazine ad, he or she must phone or write for more information. At a trade show, she or he can come to your booth, see demonstrations, and ask questions. Then the prospect can visit other manufacturers of similar products, each of whom offers a different selection of features. Such personal contact creates a sense of immediacy, and hence, shortens the buying process.

[4]"Trade Show Bureau Research Report No. 22," May 1984.

Test Market for New Products

What better way is there to make a splash with a new product than to make a big to-do at a trade show? Buyers are looking for new ideas, but at most shows they see last year's models with new colors. Buyers tire of such practices. They want to see something new! This desire provides a great opening line to use on booth-browsers: "Have you seen our multilevel, variable speed, oscillating widget? It's new!" After they've stopped to see it, you can show them last year's models with new colors, too.

Trade show introductions also provide an immediate reading on the marketability of a new product. Do the buyers really like it? Is it priced too high or too low? Does it need a new design? Will they buy it? Before making a decision on whether to produce something, I used to take prototypes of the product to shows to see how many actual orders I could get. Instead of putting together an expensive market research project, hiring a focus group, and studying volumes of numbers, just take some samples to a big show. Top buyers are paid well to know whether a product will succeed or not. If it's a winner to buyers at a trade show, it's a pretty good bet that it will be a winner in the marketplace.

Trade Shows Allow You to Compete with the Big Boys

Your company doesn't have the marketing budget of General Motors, Procter & Gamble, Sony, or Exxon? Don't worry. I don't think the U.K. does either. Based on my own observations, a small business has an equal and sometimes better marketing position at a trade show than a major company does. The reasons are simple. At a typical national or international show, there are usually hundreds of exhibitors. Because the buyers can't see everyone, they must be selective. Yes, they will make a point of seeing the companies with 10,000-square-foot, three-story-high megabooths. But, because most shows are only open a total of 25–30 hours over a few days, most buyers will give an hour to one of these large exhibitors and his 200 S.K.U. line, but that's about it. Buyers make time to walk the rest of the show, to see several small companies, because that's where they find the great new ideas. In fact, buyers will often spend *more* time in small exhibits because they won't see them in the field, unlike the big guys who call on them every week. If you prepare properly, with aggressive preshow marketing, telemarketing, an attractive exhibit, good boothmanship, and a decent location, buyers *will* visit your exhibit.

CHAPTER 2

Show Planning

Selecting the Right Show

Too many companies make the mistake of selecting a trade show merely because everyone else in the industry will be there. The smartest companies always thoroughly research a trade show before committing valuable time and money toward attending it. They establish a set of criteria to evaluate a show's potential success in light of company plans. These criteria are also used to review previously attended shows. Times and trends change; a show that was perfect for the company five years ago may no longer have the same market. A critical review of any trade show is a must before any money is committed.

Before you can begin the search for the right show or shows, there are a number of questions you need to answer:

- What are our specific objectives at a trade show?
    - Are we introducing a new product?
    - Are we shining up the corporate image? If so, what image?
    - Do we want to meet new prospects?
    - Are we interested in direct sales?
    - Do we want to build a mailing list?
    - Will we get sales leads for our field salespeople?
    - Are we researching the market for a new product or service?
    - Will we sign up new distributors?

- Can success in achieving these goals be measured?
- Who is our target market?
- Which shows now attract our best customers?
- Which sales regions are the strongest?
- Will our distributors participate in our booth?
- Can we get co-op money for trade shows?
- Which shows conform to our budget timetable?
- Which shows conform to our manufacturing timetable?
- Which shows might aid problem-sales areas?

After answering these questions, the type of show your company should be using in its marketing mix will emerge. These answers will help you establish criteria for analyzing different shows.

Locating the Right Show

Once you've drawn up your criteria, you need to find all the available shows for measuring and comparison.

If you're in a specific industry with a fairly vertical market (for example, health care, consumer electronics, fishing, LAN), you can find out the available shows through several different avenues. Contact any trade magazine in your field for a list of upcoming shows. Trade magazines usually publish an annual issue containing a schedule of trade shows. Some even do it on an issue by issue basis.

Another way is to ask your competitors what shows they exhibit at. You might be reluctant to do this, and sometimes they are reluctant to help. But, the worst they can do is not answer your question!

Public libraries contain excellent business-information resources. Most have directories of conventions and trade shows held around the world. Go to the business section and ask the reference librarians to help you find this information. The beauty of this system is that it's free!

Another good place to obtain information is in the *Tradeshow Week Data Book*. It provides information on trade and public shows held in the United States and Canada, provided the show's floor size exceeds 5,000 square feet. The only drawback is that the directory costs about $225. (The address for "Trade-show Week" is in the Appendix.)

If you're interested in shows in your region, contact your local convention center and visitors bureau. They usually have a list of all shows booked into your area, some several years in advance.

Analyze the Show

As part of the process of setting your objectives, you'll want to do a fairly complete analysis of the show, even if your company has been going to the show for years. Keep in mind that times and trends change. A show that was perfect for you five years ago may not have the same market now. A critical review of any trade show is a must before any new dollars are committed.

Show Literature

The most obvious place to start the analysis is with the sales literature and information packet provided by the show management. In it you should be able to find out about the targeted attendees and any educational sessions scheduled; it usually contains a partial list of other exhibitors, too (including your competition). These packets cover a fairly broad spectrum of information in order to appeal to a wide range of possible exhibitors. For example, the Consumer Electronics Show product categories include car stereos, clocks, computers, disco equipment, health care electronics, telephones, and prerecorded video cassettes. Read these packets carefully. Are you positive this show is for you?

Show Management

Contact the show management for more information. Ask about the estimated audience size and profile. Do they have an attendee breakdown from the last show? Get a list of last year's exhibitors. How many years has this show been going on? If it's fairly new, be careful. Ask about the management's background. Have they had successes with other shows? What type of adver-

tising and promotion will they put on? Direct mail? Trade advertising? How much? How far in advance? Who is their target
market? Is the show audited? How far in advance must you re-
serve a space? Most shows require a hefty deposit, so you might
be tying up your money for a long period of time. Can exhibitors
set up their own booths? What are normal working hours? What
is overtime? What is the height and width of the entrances to the
exhibit hall? Must hotel reservations be cleared through show
management? Are there any restrictions on noise level, lights,
entertainment? What insurance coverage does the show have?

Competitors and Other Exhibitors

What do other companies think about the show? Call your competition. You're not asking them for their cost sheets or customer list, so don't worry. Usually people are happy to share
insights into what they thought about a trade show. Ask them
where they had problems (services? unions? low attendance?
difficulty setting up?).

Ask how many companies have participated in the past. It's
important to know whether the show is dominated by large or
small space exhibitors. If there are mainly sixty-foot by eighty-
foot booths and you have a tabletop display, you might get lost in
the crowd. Conversely, if the show only has ten- and twenty-foot
spaces, and you're looking for a 2,500-square-foot island, you
may be out of place. As a general guideline for national shows,
look for 30 percent of the space to be taken up by the megabooths, and the remaining 70 percent to be occupied by the ten-
and twenty-foot spaces. Such ratios make a good balance.

Geographics

Does your company have an adequate sales staff in the local vicinity around the show? Even if it's a national show, most attendees will be from that region. If you don't have it well covered,
you may be cutting out a large number of attendees as prospects.

Timing

Is the show in conflict with any major holidays or events? I've
seen trade shows held over the Fourth of July and during the

Superbowl. Neither was a good idea. What about timing for your customers? Do you have a particular selling season? If so, be sure the show is far enough in advance to accommodate the needs of the buyers, as well as your production lines. Pay attention to buying trends, too. Ten years ago, in the toy industry, for example, orders were placed three to six months before Christmas shipping. Nowadays, it's not unusual for buying plans to start over a year ahead of time.

How does the timing fit in with your company's marketing plan? Does it fit well with new product introduction and production? Trade shows are traditionally a great place to bring out new products, but be sure to be congruent with your master plan.

Now that you've analyzed the show, you need to meld that information with your objectives. Ask yourself two questions: Based on my show analysis, will the company be able to reach its objectives? If the show analysis does not meet corporate objectives, should we go? This doesn't need to be a black and white issue. Sometimes the answer lies in how much you decide to participate. Maybe a smaller booth would prove more appropriate. Maybe the company could spend less on advertising and promotion. Perhaps you don't even need to exhibit and can accomplish some objectives by just attending, or by having a hospitality suite.

By using these sources, you should be able to glean enough show information to decide which shows are most advantageous for your company's exhibitions.

Before You Go

After you've selected the right show for your company, the real work begins. To ensure success at a trade show, it's important to put together a detailed plan of action. What's the big deal? you ask. Once you've selected the show, the steps are simple, right? All you have to do is get a booth, select a booth location, pack up some products, and go! After all, isn't that the way most companies do it?

Well, yes, that is the way most companies prepare for trade shows; that's also why most companies are just wasting their marketing resources. They might as well just stand on a street corner and hand out $50 bills.

A well-planned trade show will make you and your company successful trade show marketers. Smart companies use trade shows as an integral and effective part of their marketing mix. They know that the planning process will make or break the success of that particular show.

Unlike many projects a company undertakes, a trade show has one big advantage—a deadline. You already know the date of the exhibition, so you can work backwards from there. There should be several parts to your plan:

- Show objectives
- Preshow analysis
- Budget planning
- Target market identification
- Choosing display products
- Advertising and promotion plans
- Coordination of company personnel
- Determination of show staff and size (do you plan to train them?)
- Staff responsibilities
- Lead generation and conversion
- Postshow follow-up
- Alternatives
- Time-line for preparation

Setting Show Objectives

In the past, corporations used exhibitions and conventions as dog and pony shows. They put products on display, put on a few demonstrations, and did a lot of wining and dining. They never sold anything at the show; instead, they used it to create goodwill with customers and prospects. Unfortunately, most companies still believe that trade shows function in this manner. They don't set measurable objectives and, consequently, have no way of judging how successful a show is.

Companies still justify their corporate presence at trade shows with nebulous reasons. I'm frequently told by representatives of corporations that they attend trade shows merely because it enhances the company's image; it's good for P.R.; it supports the association and the industry; and it's necessary to maintain face with competitors. What a waste of corporate time and money. Such attitudes are old-fashioned; don't get caught up in them. If your advertising agency came to you and suggested running a very expensive direct mail campaign to your target market for no particular reason, with no specific and measurable goals in mind, would you do it? Chances are you'd start looking for a new ad agency.

In contrast, attendees go to trade shows to find solutions to company problems, to finalize purchase selections, to discover new methods and developments in the industry, and to meet with technical experts. Attendees at trade shows have learned that they need to be fiscally responsible. Anytime they spend money, they must justify it. Exhibitors need to be just as careful about supporting any expenditures. A successful trade show marketer ties in corporate objectives with the attendees' to attain specific and measurable goals and objectives.

When you set your goals, be sure to make them quantifiable by asking such questions as who? how many? and how much? Following are some objectives you might want to consider.

Total Sales

Actual sales (dollars or quantity) can be based on total on-site sales, average sales per customer, sales to existing customers, sales to new customers, sales per product, and sales achieved over a specified period of time following the show. The important thing here is to be realistic about your projections. Don't just pick numbers out of a hat. For example, if you expect to write orders with your current customers, then write down the names of those you expect to see at the show. Project what percentage of them will write orders. Fix an average dollar amount per order and multiply that by the number of orders for your total sales goal.

Qualified Lead Generation

Again, the important thing is to be realistic. If you only have two people at a time working a show that's open for a total of twenty-two hours, don't expect 1,000 leads, even if there are 100,000 attendees. It's just not going to happen. As a rule of thumb, figure that each salesperson will average six contacts per hour. The earlier example of two people working a booth for twenty-two hours brings the following results:

2 salespeople × 6 contacts/hr. = 12 total contacts/hr.
12 contacts/hr. × 22 hours   = 264 show contacts

This figure, of course, is just an estimate. Some products are conducive to higher contacts per hour and others to lower. In addition, current customers are included in the contacts per hour. So, using the above example, for every twenty-two current customers you see, you will see one less new prospect per hour. Keep in mind that this figure represents total contacts, not qualified prospects.

Minor Objectives

A trade show is a good place to introduce a current product to a new market or industry. New leads and sales are strong possibilities. Introducing a new product, service, or a new feature on an established product is also a good idea at a trade show.

Product and company image can be promoted among attendees, in the industry, and in the show's geographic vicinity. Awards and media coverage are two ways to meet these objectives.

Learn more about your competition and industry trends. Knowing what's new, who's hot, and what the most talked about product at the show is can broaden your product knowledge, making you a stronger competitor in the industry.

Trade shows allow you to conduct market research on new products. Feedback on a product's color, price, appeal, and value can be gathered. Market research among attendees can also reveal open niches. Needs that aren't being met require solutions.

Give customers a rare opportunity to meet with your corporate bigwigs and technical support staff. Often these are people your customers never meet. The connection with your customers can be strengthened by this contact.

Be sure and position the trade show as part of your overall marketing plan. Don't make the mistake of making it stand on its own. Your company has corporate objectives; tie the trade show in with them. Develop a synergistic relationship between trade shows, direct marketing, telemarketing, corporate public relations, advertising, and all other parts of the marketing mix.

Set Your Budget

The amount of money you allocate for a trade show depends largely on your objectives and how they tie in with what the show can potentially produce. Once you've made the decision to go to a show, the next step is to create a budget. This is a fairly simple, yet necessary, part of trade show planning. There are seven basic categories in the budget: space rental, the exhibit, shipping and storing, show services, personnel, advertising and promotion, and travel and entertainment. When you first start planning for the show, estimate your budget using these seven areas. (See Figure 2–1 on page 18.)

If you have past trade show records, use them to determine most of the numbers; just remember, this is only an estimate and shouldn't be used as a strict guideline. If you break down each part of the budget into more detail, expenses can be more easily determined.

Space Rental: Booth and Staff Size

Most companies don't spend any time determining how much booth space to rent. New exhibitors and small companies automatically send in for ten-foot (linear) booth spaces and then plan from there. Practically, the amount of space you rent should be directly related to your show objectives and how many people will be working the booth.

For example, you are attending a show that will be open for twenty-two hours. Informal research indicates there will be eighty current customers at the show; you set a goal of seeing 75 percent of them. You have also set an objective of generating 300 new qualified leads. Thus, the total numbers of customers and contacts you intend to see comes to 360.

Of course, there will be a certain percentage of attendees who come into your booth who won't be qualified buyers. They might have a specific need that your product line doesn't fill. They might be trade show press (yes, they are important, but they aren't qualified leads). They might just be old buddies from your past who stop by and want to talk about old times. They might be *lookie-loos;* these are the people who don't belong in the show, but come anyway. A *lookie-loo* could be a local just out for a day of entertainment or a spouse of someone working the show. It's important for you to weed these people out as quickly as possible to avoid wasting your time. Remember, at a trade show, you only have a finite number of minutes to put to profitable use; don't waste your valuable time on these people.

After you've spent a couple of minutes with an attendee, ask yourself this question, "Is the time I'm spending right now moving me closer to my show objectives?" If the answer is no, quickly move the conversation to a close. Don't worry about seemingly rude behavior. Most legitimate buyers will want to move on to exhibits that most interest them, too. Just politely say, "I'm sorry I can't spend more time with you right now. Thank you for stopping by."

No matter how quickly you get rid of an unqualified prospect, however, he or she will still take up some of your time. For example, if, during a twenty-two hour trade show, you spend two minutes apiece with three unqualified attendees per hour, you've lost 132 minutes. Over two hours of your time!

Because of these unqualified attendees, there is an *R*-Factor you need to consider; the *R* stands for "Reject." A certain per-

Figure 2–1 Estimated Exhibit Budget Form

BUDGET		
	Estimate	Actual
1. Space Rental	_____	_____
2. Exhibit	_____	_____
3. Shipping and Storing	_____	_____
4. Show Services	_____	_____
5. Personnel	_____	_____
6. Advertising and Promotion	_____	_____
7. Travel and Entertainment	_____	_____
Total	_____	_____

centage of the people you meet will automatically be rejected in the qualifying process. Therefore, the next question to ask is what percentage of people coming into the booth will be Rejects? Unless you have accurate figures from past shows, this figure will be tough to project. Several large companies have informally researched this factor and the percentages range from 16 percent to 50 percent.[1] Knowing what percentage of the attendees will be interested in your product helps determine the percentage. If you're exhibiting gourmet candy at a specialty food show, interest will be much higher than if you exhibit at a gift show. A good Reject figure to start with is 25 percent; adjust the percentage based on your knowledge of the show audience.

Let's go back to the earlier example and plug in the 25 percent R-Factor: The goal is to make 360 qualified contacts at the show. Sixty of these are current customers, so 300 new contacts must be made. If 25 percent of the contacts will be rejected, then 75 percent must be qualified. The calculations would be:

$$\text{Total contacts} \times 75\% = 300 \text{ qualified contacts}$$
$$\text{Total contacts} = 400$$

Adding the sixty current customers to this number brings the required number of attendees to 460. This figure helps determine the number of people needed to work the booth and how much booth space you need.

You've already determined that you need to make 460 contacts in twenty-two hours. That's an average of twenty-one contacts per hour. If you figure that one salesperson makes six contacts per hour, then you need four people in the booth at all times (21 divided by 6 = 3.5). Round that number up to four, or if you have to, down to three.

I highly recommend you plan on more than one shift for your salespeople. After a couple of hours working a show, a salesperson begins to become ineffective. In this example you'd need to bring eight salespeople for the two shifts.

Past research has established that each salesperson on duty needs approximately fifty square feet of unoccupied space to

[1]Informal interviews conducted with show managers of several companies. Results are dependent on size of show as well as whether the show market is deemed horizontal or vertical.

work in.[2] In addition, the exhibitor must determine the amount of space to be occupied by the booth itself, products, tables, and chairs; figure another 50 percent of that space for such things. So for every salesperson on duty, you need seventy-five square feet of booth space. Four salespeople would require 300 square feet.

Once you've determined the number of people you need on duty and the space required to accommodate them, you can project how much to budget for the space rental.

Let's be frank, though. These calculations are designed to reflect ideal situations. Not all of us can afford a 300-square-foot exhibit. But these formulas do provide a checks and balances system for your objectives. Are you projecting to get 300 new contacts, when you can only budget for a 100-square-foot booth? Maybe you should reevaluate your goals to avoid being disappointed by the postshow results.

Don't be discouraged if you can only project 120 new leads at a show. What percentage of those leads will you be able to close? If you were only able to get ten new customers, how much will they be worth to you over the next ten years? Be realistic about your objectives, but also recognize that trade shows can be very cost effective.

Exhibit Expenses

Lots of questions can be asked here. Do you even have an exhibit? How old is it? Is it big enough to handle your space requirements? How much refurbishing does it need? Do the design and colors still fit within the corporate image and your objectives? Is it a custom or a portable? Do you need a custom or a portable? I'll get into more detail about the actual design and construction of your booth in Chapter 3. Only the budget requires consideration here. There are six areas that need to be addressed:

Design and construction. Do you require a custom booth? If so, then you'll need to have it designed. There are two ways to do this—each having a different impact on your budget.

---

[2]Approximate figure for salesperson plus attendee. Calculations are shown in the section on "Booth Design."

You can hire an exhibit design specialist. This is expensive, but if your budget allows, a custom designed booth will help you more easily reach your goals. The specialist should design your booth for easy shipping, long life, and ease in setup. Exhibit Surveys, under the commission of the Trade Show Bureau, determined that a new custom construction costs an average of $801 per linear foot for a backwalled display and $41 per square foot for an island or peninsula display.[3]

The best way to find a good designer or exhibit house is to ask other exhibitors. When you're at a show, look for well-designed booths, and then ask for the names of its designers. If you can't find one that way, look in the yellow pages or contact the Exhibit Designers and Producers Association for a list of members.

Exhibit Designers And Producers Association
611 E. Wells Street
Milwaukee, WI 53202
414/276-3372

If you have designers on staff capable of designing and constructing a booth to fit your requirements, great. But be careful that they do, in fact, know what they're doing. Designing an easy-to-build, easy-to-ship, and easy-to-take-down booth is no simple feat. If you're doing it in house just to save money, you're doing it for the wrong reason.

Graphics. If you're designing or buying a new exhibit, it will come with new graphics; if you're not, make sure your graphics are up to date. Although it's not cheap to update your graphics regularly for each show, it's necessary. Ask your designer for an estimate.

Refurbishing. Trade shows are hard on exhibits. During setup, tear down, and shipping, exhibits get banged around. No matter how sturdy they are, they take a beating and eventually show it. You should plan to refurbish your exhibit on an annual basis. Remember, your exhibit is your showcase. The first thing people see when walking down an aisle is the exhibit. If it's in bad

---

[3]These figures are from the "Trade Show Bureau's Research Report No. 2060," November 1988.

shape—dirty, worn out, broken at the edges, partially lit from broken light fixtures—then that is the impression your current and future customers will have of your company. Contact your exhibit house for the costs to refurbish.

Products for display. Your company may build the products for display, but you've still got to pay for them. Put it in your budget.

Booth rental. You might not want to buy an exhibit. Maybe you don't know if you want to commit to trade shows long term, or perhaps your company has committed its only booth to another show. The good news on renting is you don't worry about shipping, setting up, tearing down, or storage costs. The bad news is that rental exhibits are boring and will not stand out during a busy show.

Used-booth purchase. Companies are always trading in or selling their old booths when designing new ones. Sometimes you can find a well-designed exhibit that is functional for your use and reasonably priced. Be prepared to spend some money on refurbishing, and make sure it's strong enough to display your products!

Keep in mind the projected life span of your booth. If you use it for more than one show (which I hope you do), then amortize the cost over all the applicable shows. For example, if you invest $10,000 in a new booth and plan to use it in five different shows, then put down $2,000 as the cost of the booth on your budget.

Shipping

I won't go into a complete discussion on transportation, but here is a brief description. Most exhibits are shipped one of three ways: common carrier, van line, and air freight. Each has its advantages and disadvantages.

Common carrier. The biggest advantage for a common carrier is it's usually the cheapest way to go. The major disadvantage is that the common carrier is not designed to carry trade show exhibits, but to merely move freight from place to place. Timing is also not exact; allow more time to get to the show. If you know how many cubic feet the exhibit covers and its weight, you can get quotes by phone.

Van line. Most of us relate van lines to moving household goods; however, most large van line companies have special departments for handling trade show exhibits. They understand your needs and will work closely with you. The disadvantage is cost, although deregulation has brought costs down somewhat. In the long run, this is the best shipping choice. You can get rough quotes by phone, just as common carriers do.

Air carrier. If it absolutely, positively has to be there overnight, or if your company is having a contest to see who can foolishly spend the most money, then use an air carrier. Otherwise, stay away.

Show Services

Whether you like it or not, the odds are you'll have to hire some type of service and if you use any services at trade shows, then you will have to work with unions.

If you need labor for setting up your exhibit, get an independent contractor to hire and supervise setup. You'll be provided a supervisor with whom you can work and you'll probably get a prescreened group from the labor pool. This type of organization will give you higher quality performance and fewer problems. Be sure and order this help well in advance of the show and also provide the show organizer with written notification that you will be working with an independent and authorized labor source.

Pay attention to what time of day you will be using labor. Overtime begins after a certain time of day during the week and is in effect all weekend. Labor is expensive and does not charge by fractions of the hour. Labor contracts usually provide for a two-man crew with a minimum charge of one hour per man. Costs add up quickly; so if you can set up during a weekday, you'll save money.

If you don't want to work with an independent contractor, it's doubly important to order labor in advance. If you wait until you get to the show, you might be stuck with fill-in labor, since all the professional labor has been preassigned. Many people suspect that theft and attitude problems come mainly from fill-ins. Order early.

Be careful to coordinate the job assignment for booth setup with the delivery of your exhibit. It's a common sight at a show to see labor sitting around an empty booth waiting for the exhibit to arrive. Don't worry though; they're patient about waiting. After all, even if they're not working you're still paying them—a lot.

If things don't go exactly as you plan, be patient and try to work things out. If there's a major problem with labor, go to the Official Service Contractor and discuss it with them. Don't ask for trouble by getting upset; you're on their turf.

Of course, if you've got a custom display, you don't have any choice. You'll be using union help to put it up. But if you've got a small portable exhibit, then how do you get around having to hire expensive union help?

Technically, you probably can't. But there is an unwritten rule that usually applies. It's called the Half-Hour Rule. What this means is that if you can hand carry your exhibit into the exhibition hall, and set it up *by yourself* in less than thirty minutes, then the unions usually won't bother you. I say usually, because I've been in certain convention centers (who shall remain nameless to protect my future participation) where the unions wouldn't even let me put up a tabletop display. Fortunately, most halls aren't like that. Most union workers are hard-working, conscientious people who want to do a good job, if you give them a chance.

Besides using labor for helping in the booth setup and breakdown, there are a number of other services available—electrical, furniture rentals, telephone, carpeting, signage, cleaning, security, computer rentals, and photographer. Again, I recommend you contract as far in advance as is possible for any services you require.

A word about security. Don't ever assume your products are safe. If there's any doubt, get some security. If your products are small enough to fit in a security cage, rent one. If not, get a guard. True, it's another expense, but it's a lot less expensive to hire a security guard than to be at a show with little or nothing to exhibit.

There is the classic story of the exhibitor who didn't hire a security guard for his expensive consumer electronics. The reason? The large exhibit across the aisle from him had several guards watching the display, so he assumed they'd keep an eye on his. The next morning he arrived to an empty booth. All his products had been stolen. And the security guards in his neighbor's booth claimed they didn't see a thing.

Personnel

Several years ago, a mentor of mine, Thad Turk, taught me a lesson about the value of people in business. He said, "A company with a first-class product and second-class personnel will probably fail. But a company with a second-class product and first-class people will undoubtedly succeed." If I were to translate that into trade show terms, it would come out something like this: "An exhibit with a first-class product and first-class booth, but with a second-class floor staff will probably fail. An exhibit with a second-class product and second-class booth, but with a first-class floor staff will undoubtedly succeed." Unfortunately (or fortunately, depending on how you look at it), most companies don't pay much attention to their booth staff for trade shows. They simply assign certain "lucky" people to work the next show.

Not all companies put personnel as a category in their budget. I believe it's important, even though it is actually an indirect cost. It doesn't directly come out of your show budget, but it does cost your company to have those people there.

Wages/salaries. Estimate the cost of each salesperson's time to your company. If you want to be really accurate, then include all compensation—salary, commission, bonus, and benefits. Total this up for a year and divide by 230 (the average number of workdays after subtracting vacation, holidays, and some sick days). This gives you the average cost per day for that person.

For example, Scott M. makes $30,000 base pay, plus another $10,000 in commissions and bonuses annually. His benefits (health insurance and company car) total another $7,500. His total compensation package is $47,500 per year. Divide the

$47,500 by 230, and Scott costs approximately $207 per day. If Scott spends five days at the trade show, his total cost is $1,035.

Do this simple calculation for each person going to the show to obtain the total personnel time figure. If you don't know or can't get exact compensation figures, then estimate their salary and benefits. The important thing is to have something down in this category.

Outside help. Sometimes you need extra people. Whether it's a magician, an actor, or someone hired to demonstrate your products, be sure and project the cost into your budget.

Advertising and Promotion

As I said at the beginning of this chapter, the average exhibitor rents booth space, puts up the booth, hangs a sign, and then waits around for the buyers to flock in. That's the way we'd all like it to happen, but it doesn't.

The few days that the trade show is open represent only one-third of the total trade show marketing process. The other two-thirds are preshow planning and postshow follow-up. The entire marketing event, if done correctly, takes several months.

Advertising and promotion are an integral part of the total picture. In a study conducted for the Trade Show Bureau,[4] Robert T. Wheeler, Jr., identified eight factors influencing attendees' decisions to visit specific exhibits.

1. Obligation: 25 percent. Based on past business activities or relationships attendees feel an obligation to visit.
2. Habit: 23 percent. The attendee has been visiting a particular exhibit for several years, and as long as the exhibitor is there, he or she'll stop by.
3. Personal invitation: 15 percent. When a targeted prospect received a personal invitation from a sales or corporate representative, he or she made a point to visit.
4. Trade journal publicity: 12 percent. Make sure to get as many news and feature stories in trade journals as possible.

[4]These figures came from Robert T. Wheeler, Jr.'s, survey in the "Trade Show Bureau Research Report No. 13," July 1982.

5. Advertising: 9 percent. Advertise your products and show location in preshow issues of the trade journal.
6. Mail invitations: 9 percent. Although not as effective as personal invitations, they still bring a good response. Send information and invitations to as many qualified prospects as possible.
7. Recommendations from associates: 3 percent. You can have an effect on this factor.
8. Not sure: 3 percent. These are the same people who voted "Undecided" in the Pepsi Challenge.

In my opinion, exhibitors have a lot of control over numbers three, four, five, and six, and partial control over number seven; that's control of 49 percent of all reasons attendees visit a selected exhibit.

Also include in your budget any on-site handouts, giveaways, press kits, or anything else that falls under this category. I'll discuss all advertising and promotion in more detail in Chapter 5.

Travel and Entertainment

Like the personnel category, most companies don't figure the cost of travel and entertainment into their show budget. But it's still there.

Ask your travel agent for the airline and hotel figures. Then estimate how much entertainment (do you have a hospitality suite?) you need to include.

Now Put It All Together

Once you've put numbers down for each of these seven areas of your budget, it's time to put it all together. Use Figure 2–2 on pages 28–29 as a guideline for developing your own customized budget.

Who Is Your Target Market?

I have a sign over my desk given to me by a good friend, Jim Cathcart, author of *Relationship Selling*, and 1988–89 President

Figure 2–2 Customized Exhibit Budget Form

EXHIBIT BUDGET

Name of Show _____

Date of Show _____

Item	Budget	Actual
1. Space Rental	_____	_____
2. Exhibit Expenses		
a. Design and construction	_____	_____
b. Graphics	_____	_____
c. Refurbishing	_____	_____
d. Products for display	_____	_____
e. Booth rental	_____	_____
f. Used booth purchase	_____	_____
g. Total exhibit expenses	_____	_____
3. Shipping and Storage	_____	_____
a. Freight	_____	_____
b. Drayage	_____	_____
c. Exhibit storage	_____	_____
d. Total shipping and storage	_____	_____
4. Show Services	_____	_____
a. On-site labor (set up)	_____	_____
b. On-site labor (tear down)	_____	_____
c. Electrical	_____	_____
d. Furniture rentals	_____	_____
e. Misc. rentals (plants, etc.)	_____	_____
f. Telephone	_____	_____
g. Carpeting	_____	_____
h. Signage	_____	_____
i. Cleaning	_____	_____
j. Security	_____	_____
k. Computer rental	_____	_____

l. Photography   _____   _____

m. Imprinter rental   _____   _____

n. Florist   _____   _____

o. Audiovisual equipment   _____   _____

p. Other   _____   _____

q. Total show services   _____   _____

5. Personnel   _____   _____

   a. Wages/salary   _____   _____

   b. Outside help   _____   _____

   c. Total personnel   _____   _____

6. Advertising and Promotion   _____   _____

   a. Preshow advertising and
      promotion   _____   _____

   b. On-site advertising and
      promotion   _____   _____

   c. Postshow advertising
      and promotion   _____   _____

   d. Total advertising and
      promotion   _____   _____

7. Travel and Entertainment   _____   _____

   a. Airfares   _____   _____

   b. Housing   _____   _____

   c. Staff meals   _____   _____

   d. Client meals and
      entertainment   _____   _____

   e. Hospitality suite   _____   _____

   f. Miscellaneous   _____   _____

   g. Total travel and
      entertainment   _____   _____

Total Show Expenses   _____   _____

of the 3,000-member National Speakers Association. On that sign is a single, simple sentence:

> The Purpose of Business Is to Identify, Develop and Serve the Most Appropriate Clientele.

I put that sign over my desk so I'd read it every day. It not only tells me, in general terms, why I'm in business, but who buys my products and services—the most appropriate clientele.

In today's marketplace, if you don't know who, what, and where your true prospects are, or if you fail to go after them as individuals, you will lose ground to competitors who do.

The thing to keep in mind is that, with few exceptions, not every attendee at a trade show is a potential prospect. Most shows just aren't designed that way. In fact, according to a Trade Show Bureau Report, approximately 16 percent of all attendees at an average show will be qualified prospects for you.[5]

As mentioned earlier, people attend trade shows to look for solutions to specific problems, finalize selections for purchase after the show, identify any new methods or developments in their field, and meet with technical experts. Each of these reasons is personal to each prospective buyer. And because they are personal, there is no such thing as a universal product, that is, one for which every attendee is a buyer.

Do you already know who your target market is? Great! Then all you have to do is put it on paper. Define those customers or clients so that your show staff will also be able to identify them.

Defining Your Target Market

If individuals make up your target market, consider the following questions:

- Are they male, female, or both?
- Are they married, single, or divorced?
- How old are they?
- What is their net worth?

---

[5] This figure came from the "Trade Show Bureau Research Report No. 3," April 1979.

- Where do they live?
- How much do they travel?
- How much education do they have?
- What are their favorite sports?
- How many kids do they have?
- Do they own computers?

    If your target market is a business:

- What is its sales volume?
- How many employees?
- What industry is it in?
- What type of phone system does it use?
- How are customers reached? Direct sales? Telemarketing? Direct mail?
- Does it have a fleet of cars? Are they leased?
- Is it in mail order?
- Does it use advertising specialties?

The questions in these lists are by no means complete, representing only a sample of the type of questions you should ask about your target market. The idea is to stimulate you to ask detailed questions in order to identify your ideal client or customer. Once you are able to do this, you are in a better position to find your prospects at the trade show and attract them into your booth.

A Preshow Time Line

The Japanese taught the Americans a valuable way to handle inventory. It's called "Just-in-Time." The whole idea is that production parts are not brought into the factory until the assembly line absolutely needs them. This practice saves on space and on the cost of keeping a large inventory of spare parts. Just-in-Time is a wonderful method, requiring a tremendous amount of coordination with suppliers to provide the products when they are needed. Unfortunately, Just-in-Time preparation is a common practice among trade show exhibitors, although it is not usually intentional.

The typical scenario happens about four weeks before a show. The boss's internal alarm clock goes off, and all of a sudden the trade show, left to the last minute, escalates in importance. Many things can, and usually do, go wrong: the graphics are wrong; the booth is worn out; new products and catalogs aren't ready; hotels are booked; Supersaver airfares are sold out. Sound familiar? Excedrin headache number nine, right?

Scenarios such as these exemplify why it's so important to develop a timetable for your preshow planning. Planning should begin as early as possible. Some companies plan eighteen months to two years ahead of time. Although you may not always have the luxury of planning that far in advance, my recommendation is twelve months.

Twelve Months before Show

- Evaluate available shows for selection.
- Select space and send in contract with deposit.
- Analyze the show. Who will attend? What is the general show theme?
- Begin planning show. Assemble your Show Team for a planning session. Develop your objectives. Put them on paper.
- Establish a show budget.

Eleven Months before Show

- Make hotel reservations. Be sure and allow for inevitable personnel changes. Hotels don't like that, but then, they overbook, too, don't they?
- Make airline reservations.
- Assign booth personnel. Remember, this is not a training ground for rookies, nor is it a vacation.

Ten Months before Show

- Begin planning display. Can your old one be refurbished, or do you need a new one?
- Consult with display builders.
- Check show regulations to make sure your plans are within procedures.

Nine Months before Show

- Finalize booth design. Does it need show management approval? Don't just arbitrarily build an exhibit and assume you can use it. Make sure you have permission to put it up.
- Have another planning session with your show team.

Eight Months before Show

- Review your budget. Make sure it is still realistic.
- Consult with display builder. Make sure they are on schedule with you.

Seven Months before Show

- Work with show team on products for display. Does this need to be coordinated with your production or design departments?
- Bring in the advertising department. Update them on the project and get them started planning publicity and promotion tied into general show theme.

Six Months before Show

- Consult with display builder on status from their end. Finalize any design and graphics not already done.
- Check on any company literature to be used for show. Is it appropriate for this particular show? Do you have sufficient quantity?
- Order any supplies and equipment needed for the show.
- Contact restaurants in trade show city for reservations for each night during show. Make enough for show staff and guests.

Five Months before Show

- Review Exhibitor Kit (if it has arrived) sent from the show management. Fill out any forms requesting product information, program listing, or promotional materials.
- Fill out advanced registration forms for all your personnel.
- Meet with Show Team for updates and status reports.

Four Months before Show

- Work with advertising department to send out press releases, new product introductions, and promotional materials to news media.
- Meet with van line representative to arrange for shipment of all exhibit materials, sample products, display, and literature.
- Arrange for any floor selling training.

Three Months before Show

- Submit all necessary forms for services (furniture, carpets, cleaning, electricity, labor, telephone, computer, security, etc.). Prepay if possible to get preshow discounts.
- Begin preshow marketing campaign to stimulate attendance.
- Meet with Show Team for updates and status reports.

Two Months before Show

- Reconfirm hotel and airline reservations.
- Finalize booth personnel, schedules, and assignments.
- Put together your company's personalized exhibit staff handbook (covered in Chapter 3).
- Meet with Show Team for updates and status reports.
- Accelerate your preshow marketing program. Mail personalized invitations to prospects and customers.

One Month before Show

- Put up your display for inspection and last-minute corrections.
- Double-check to make sure show service forms were sent.
- Insure your exhibit.
- Work with your transportation people for a final check on all arrangements.
- Ship exhibit materials, display, and literature to arrive on the first day space is available for receiving shipments.
- Preshow training programs for show staff should be confirmed.
- Put together all necessary office and sales supplies.
- Get traveler's checks for any on-site payments.

On Site before Show

- Install exhibit on the first day your space is available. Be prepared to handle any last-minute problems.
- Confirm all show orders for labor and rentals.
- Conduct preshow training and rehearsals.
- Take care of any last-minute crises.

During Show

- Conduct daily meetings to evaluate show progress and assess any changes needed.
- Keep the booth clean.
- Arrange for exhibit tear down after show.
- Arrange for next year's space, if possible.

After Show

- Oversee tear down and packing.
- Evaluate results of leads generated at show and distribute leads as soon as possible.
- Evaluate overall company performance.
- Begin new planning timetable for next year's show.

It takes some time to fill out all necessary information and project deadlines, but you'll be glad you did. As the show approaches, you won't have all those last-minute rush orders to sweat over. By having this time line posted on your wall or in a trade show workbook, you'll be able to refer to it easily, maintain a schedule, and show how professional you are.

CHAPTER 3

Coordinating the Show

The Exhibit Planning Handbook

Along with your time line, one of the most valuable aids to your show success is the *Exhibit Planning Handbook*. This notebook will keep everything organized and understandable. Get yourself a three-ring binder (preferably at least two inches wide) and divide it into eight sections:

Planning

In this section include your time line, budget, notes, or minutes of Show Team meetings, show objectives, and any other material pertinent to the planning process.

Exhibit

This section contains any information about the exhibit and the graphics, including setup instructions, pictures or line drawings of what the final setup should look like, how to make quick repairs, and who to call for emergency help.

Show Services

This section holds copies of all show orders—labor, electricity, rentals, telephone, cleaning, and the like. Also have photocopies of any checks written for these services.

Promotion

This section includes copies of ads, direct mail pieces, mailing lists, ad schedules, and anything used in the marketing and advertising campaign for the show.

Shipping

Include copies of bills of lading, the PRO number or air bill number, the trailer number or flight number, the name of the delivering carrier (if different from your original carrier), the telephone number of your carrier representative in your home town, the telephone number of the carrier representative at the show site, transfer points and phone numbers, and the telephone number of the terminal show destination.

On Duty

This section includes all information related to your show staff, show training, and the like. Include a complete copy of the *Exhibit Staff Manual* outlined later in this chapter.

Lead Fulfillment

Include copies of lead generation forms and any plans and objectives on lead conversion in this section.

Miscellaneous

Place under "Miscellaneous" anything related to the trade show that isn't included in the previously described categories.

By compiling this information and putting it in your own *Master Exhibit Planning Manual* you will be accomplishing three important objectives:

1. You will have everything conveniently located in one place. You can take it with you to the show or give it to whomever is in charge at the show. Not only does this organization make your job easier, but it makes you look more professional, too.
2. Any postshow report you make to your boss can include this manual. Your boss will be impressed.
3. The manual is a historical document that can serve as a guideline for future shows.

At this point, it is important to consider the question of staff coordination and the use of an *Exhibit Staff Manual.*

Coordinating All Personnel

Show planning involves a number of people—corporate management, exhibit manager, sales manager, and sales staff. But don't forget your other support staff—the people back in the office. You need to include them in the planning as well as the implementation. During the show's planning stages, especially during meetings, include those who might have some valuable input and those who will be affected by the show. This includes secretaries, assistants, production people, design staff, marketing and advertising personnel, and also upper management who might not be going to the show. Be sure everybody understands the importance of the show, as well as the show objectives. By doing so, you'll get more complete cooperation and smoother teamwork. This, in turn, makes for better communication within your company and better service outside.

The Exhibit Staff Manual

Every person who will be going to the show should get an *Exhibit Staff Manual.* Much like a playbook for a professional football team, the staff manual includes the who, what, when, where, and why of the show. Following are some of the areas you'll want to cover:

- Who will be working the booth
- Where they will be staying
- A map showing the convention hall and vicinity
- Name, addresses, and phone numbers of show facilities
- How messages will be handled
- Explanations of preshow advertising and promotions
- A map of the hall layout with your exhibit location
- A diagram of your exhibit layout

- A list of products to be displayed
- Staff work schedule
- Who will be attending conferences and when
- New product information
- Product pricing structure
- Corporate objectives for the show
- Individual job assignments
- Personal objectives for staff members to fill out
- How to qualify prospects
- How to handle sales leads
- What printed collateral will be distributed
- Information about daily staff meetings
- Information about entertaining customers/prospects
- How to deal with the press
- Break down and departure procedures
- Return shipping

This handbook should be highly confidential. Make sure that everybody receiving one understands the importance of knowing where it is at all times. Stress the importance of not leaving a manual lying around for prying eyes.

Designing and Building Your Exhibit

So your last exhibit had a rotating stage for the magician, laser beams streaking overhead, and special cubbyholes for Las Vegas showgirls who stuck cute little fuzzy birds on the shoulders of every person passing by? Gee, I don't understand why you didn't get any sales, either. Be serious, folks. Such antics are useless.

Good booth design focuses on the product and increases legitimate show traffic, without ridiculous gimmicks. If there is a main purpose for your booth, it's that it should attract the specific prospects you want to talk to. This goal should be foremost in your mind when designing an exhibit.

I highly recommend using a legitimate exhibit house to help you design and build your exhibit; nonetheless, you will want to be as prepared for them as possible. By understanding the various aspects of booth design and how they relate to your own needs, you will be in a better position to communicate with the designer.

Booth Size

This factor depends on your show budget, desired objectives, the available show space, and personnel capabilities.

Budget is the biggest factor. Unfortunately, many of us don't have the luxury of an unlimited budget and exhibits range in cost from as low as $1,000 (for a small tabletop with no graphics) to as high as $1 million (for an elaborate custom megabooth). Your budget will probably fall somewhere in between.

Like most of us, you probably don't control your budget and have to settle for a ten-foot display. That's okay; just keep in mind that the size of your exhibit has a direct bearing on the results of your show. For example, if your major objective at a show is to generate new leads, the amount of actual leads you can generate will be affected by this limited space.

An exhibit generally occupies approximately 30 percent of your available space. In a ten-foot by ten-foot booth (100 square feet), your exhibit will cover approximately thirty square feet. That leaves only seventy square feet for exhibitors and attendees. The average person will use approximately twenty-five square feet of personal space. (This number comes from our penchant, as human beings, to "own" a certain amount of space around us, usually extending as far as the length of our arm. Ever heard of an "arm's length transaction"?)

By going back to our high school math, we remember that the area of a circle is represented by the formula:

$$Area = pi \times (radius\ of\ circle)\ squared$$

In this example, pi is equal to 3.14, and the radius is equal to 3. By inserting these values, we now have:

$$Area = 3.14 \times (3)\ squared = 3.14 \times 9 = 28.26\ sq.\ ft.$$

If you have seventy square feet of space available for people, at twenty-five square feet per person, then approximately three people fit in your booth, including salespeople. With two salespeople in this booth, it would still be very crowded.

Now, by assuming your salespeople average six contacts per hour for a thirty-hour show, your total contacts possible for the show would be 360.

2 salespeople × 6 contacts/hr. × 30 hours = 360 total show contacts

This figure is totally independent of the size of the show. It doesn't matter whether the show attracts 100,000 people or 1,000 people. With a ten-foot booth, you can only contact 360 attendees.

If you're fortunate enough to have a large budget, you can work backwards from your objectives to determine the size of your exhibit. If you want 3,000 contacts, divide that number by the total show hours (we'll use thirty again); that's 100 contacts per hour. If salespeople make six contacts per hour, then you need seventeen salespeople (100 divided by 6). Seventeen salespeople each occupy twenty-five square feet, for a total of 425 square feet. Of course, if each of them is working with an attendee, you need to double the required space to 850 square feet, which equals 70 percent of the exhibit space. The other 30 percent contains the exhibit itself. By extrapolating these numbers, you need a booth of approximately 1,200 square feet to accommodate your objectives, a booth approximately forty feet by thirty-four feet. That's a big booth.

Booth Location

This debate rages on. Most experienced show people will tell you that the best location in a show is near the front and center of the exhibition hall. To close the debate once and for all, the Trade Show Bureau studied the effect of booth location on exhibit performance and impact.[1] The analysis showed that an exhibit's location does not affect booth traffic, exhibit performance, and the impact on an audience. The result of this study, however, hasn't reduced debate, and I still recommend common sense when deciding on location. Here are some factors for you to consider:

[1]"Trade Show Bureau Research Report No. 20," October 1983.

- Look for the traffic flow. Regardless of the results of the study, it's probably still a good idea to try and be near an entrance or exit.
- Don't be afraid of your competitors; you're all in the same place, anyway. Good buyers will examine all of you, and if you have a tremendous advantage over your competitors, why not get close to them? It provides an opportunity to toot your own horn.
- If you use gas or water, get near the source.
- Get to know the show management. They'll have a good feel for traffic flow and can help you select a location.
- Avoid dead ends; people just don't like them.
- Avoid food concession areas. The lines tend to back up and you certainly don't want them blocking your booth. Also, unless you've got a generic product, you're only trying to attract your specific target market, not every Tom, Dick, and Sherry.
- Watch for posts and columns located smack in the middle of your booth. Ask the show management for a floor plan.
- Watch for level changes. You won't want to work on a ramp during the whole show.

What Is Your Message?

Too often companies get caught in the identity trap at trade shows. They design their booth with huge signs displaying the corporate logo and company name. Unless your name is very recognizable, like IBM, Sony, Weyerhaeuser, or General Motors, it's not going to stop anyone. Your message should be simple and effective. It should list a benefit to your specific target market, so attendees will stop to learn more about how you can help them. The structure shouldn't compete with the message, nor should it overpower the all-important products on display.

What Are the Purposes of the Booth?

How do you plan to use the booth? Will it be used just once for a special occasion, such as the introduction of a new product or the celebration of a corporate anniversary? A custom design might suit such purposes. Or do you plan to use it fifteen times a year for the next five years? If so, you need to build something durable, easy to transport, and easy to assemble.

What other uses do you have for your display? Will it be stored between shows or will it be used in your office lobby? Maybe you'll take it to shopping mall shows as well as industry trade shows.

The more you can define the uses for your exhibit in advance, the fewer headaches you'll experience later.

What Type of Exhibit Do You Want?

There are several different types of exhibits available for consideration:

- Tabletop. These exhibits are designed for display atop a six- or eight-foot table. They're easy to set up, take down, and transport. They are also the least expensive.
- Portable display. Like the tabletop exhibit, these are easy to set up, take down, and transport; their advantage is they stand alone. A portable is easily carried and its size allows it to be checked as luggage on an airplane.
- Modular display. This is one where the structural elements are interchangeable, providing maximum flexibility in arrangement and size. A twenty-foot display, for example, can be broken down into two ten-foot displays.
- Custom display. This is an exhibit specifically designed and built for the user. It is usually the most expensive of all displays built.
- Rental display. A complete package offered through a trade show on a rental basis.
- Used display. A previously owned and used display.

The type of exhibit you use depends largely on your needs and budget. Be forewarned; it's easy to buy more than you really need. Determine your objectives and budget before you sit down with an exhibit house or independent designer, then stick to your plan.

Design Considerations

When designing a new booth, consider how to put your products in a good light. Colors should be neutral, not loud. You don't want the booth competing with the product. Also, bright colors tend to show wear and tear more easily. Use minimal graphics and make them large and easy to read. You only have a few seconds to attract attendees. Keep the message simple and impactful.

Good overall lighting is a must. People's eyes turn toward lighted objects. Highlight your message and products with good lighting.

Use counters for display. People are much more comfortable working at countertop level. It's easier for their eyes to look at and they don't have to bend over. Demonstrations are also easier to do from chest-high level.

Make sure the booth is clean and attractive. Does it pick up dirt easily? Is it easy to clean and refurbish? A clean booth is much more attractive to your visitors.

Display large photos. It's much more eye-appealing and attractive to use a single large photo, compared to a series of smaller pictures.

Can you use audiovisual? Can audiovisual be incorporated into the design for maximum impact and memorability?

Demonstrations are a great way to attract your target market. Does your display allow enough space for effective demonstrations and is it designed to enhance the demonstration?

Weight. Is it easily transportable? Can you carry it yourself or do you need to have it shipped by van lines?

Carpeting. Do you need your own carpeting or can you rent one at each show that will match your exhibit?

Lead Generation and Fulfillment

Several years ago, when I was national sales manager for a Japanese toy company, I made sure we participated in as many regional and national trade shows as possible. I was convinced that trade shows were a great place to get new leads. We traveled around the country exhibiting and talking to thousands of enthusiastic prospects. And, like most companies, we compiled business cards and sent them off to our independent reps with visions of millions of dollars in orders rolling in. To our surprise (and chagrin), the avalanche of new customers never materialized. In fact, over several months, they barely represented a trickle. Having invested a tremendous amount of time and money to go to those shows, we were understandably upset and confused. What happened to all those enthusiastic prospects? Where were the orders we expected?

We knew an analysis of the situation was necessary. Like any good sales manager, I blamed the sales reps. After all, I slaved at all those shows, collecting business cards, sleeping in airports, living out of my suitcase, just so I could send them thousands of leads. Something had to be wrong with these guys. So I called the reps and asked what happened to all those great leads? Where were the sales? The response from the reps surprised me:

"I drove all over my territory to see the first six people on the list. They had no intention of buying anything. Because it was a total waste of my time, I tossed the rest of the leads in one of my desk drawers."

"I learned a long time ago that trade show leads aren't worth anything. I never bother to follow them up. I've got better things to do with my time."

"The list of leads you gave me contained no information about those prospects. How was I to know what you showed them or discussed at the show? It would be just like making cold calls."

"By the time you sent the leads to me, these people had already made their decisions. You waited too long."

At first I was upset with my reps, feeling they were just plain lazy. I blamed them for the failure of the trade show program. Fortunately, I realized there was something to their statements. Maybe I was missing something.

I began a more in-depth study of trade show sales leads. I asked the reps to tell me what information they wanted about leads. What could a show staff do to make leads more valuable? What would turn those leads into sales?

From talking with the reps, I learned that we needed to pay more attention to providing them with qualified inquiries. I realized there were actually two ways to qualify a show inquiry. The first was to continue working shows the way we had, and then hire a telemarketing firm to call all the leads generated to prioritize them in order of buying time frame. Then we would send only qualified leads to reps. The second, and most expedient, way to qualify inquiries is to have the floor staff do it right at the show. We felt this was the best way to go, but more information was still needed.

I spoke with current customers, asking them what they looked for at trade shows. How could an exhibitor know whether they were going to buy or not? I talked to our reps, asking them what information they needed to help close the sale. I talked with show managers, asking for more information about the attendees at various shows. I called the Trade Show Bureau and asked for information about how to make shows more effective. I even talked to other exhibitors (including competitors), asking them how they handled new leads.

This informal, but enlightening, survey led me to a number of insights and conclusions:

1. Generating leads is by far the biggest reason why companies exhibit at trade shows. A Trade Show Bureau Research Report showed that 86 percent of all companies at trade shows are there to generate new leads.[2]
2. Everybody in the loop must buy into your program for it to be a success. Qualified lead generation and fulfillment require the cooperation of the exhibit and field staff, the sales reps (whether in house or independent), and the buyers.
3. A business card is not a qualified lead. Although it does not take a mental giant to figure this out, many companies still use this method to collect leads. I used to be guilty of it. Lead forms need to be designed to include enough room for proper data collection. And don't plan on writing information on the back of business cards. They just aren't big enough.
4. The exhibit and field staff require proper training to approach, qualify, and rate prospects during a very short time frame at the show. So short, in fact, I now call it "The $9^{1}/_{2}$ Minute Sales Call."
5. The sales reps need to be prepared to follow up and report on qualified trade show leads. Lead follow-up begins in the home office, using direct mail and telemarketing. Leads should be followed up in a timely manner and then dispensed to the proper rep.

[2]"Trade Show Bureau Research Report No. 2050," July 1988.

6.   Once a lead has been assigned to a rep, a tracking system must be implemented to encourage and demand timely follow-through.
7.   A word processing system is a must for immediate show follow-up, field assignments, and future communications.

Once I came to these conclusions, we were able to implement a more effective trade show lead conversion program. The first thing we did was outline a show lead form. From my research we were able to determine what information was needed on the form:

1.   Complete identification of the prospect, including name, company, address, phone, fax number (if available), and company profile.
2.   Specific product interest and area of use.
3.   Budget and buying time frame.
4.   Other possible buying influencers. Who else might be involved in the decision-making process?
5.   Comments from prospect—specific objections, concerns, special situations, requests, and so on.
6.   Name of trade show and dates held.
7.   Information for postshow follow-up. Do they need a personal call? Did they request literature? Do they need a sample?
8.   Personal comment about prospect. Did he wear a great looking tie at the show? Did she mention her recent vacation to Europe? This information is used in follow-up letters to add a personal touch.
9.   Name and signature of person filling out lead form.
10. A rating system for handling and prioritizing inquiries. We came up with a simple 1,2,3 system for rating leads. A 1-rated lead was super hot and required immediate follow-up. A 2-rated prospect was considered warm. We would send requested literature with a cover letter, but would follow up with a phone call to requalify before making a personal sales call. All 3-rated contacts were put on our in-house mailing list; if they showed more interest, we would elevate them to 2-status. We only sent 1- and 2-rated leads to our reps. Using this rating system also helped us set objectives for each show. For example, we might go to

one show with a goal of reaching twenty new 1-rated leads and 150 new 2-rated leads.

11.   Follow-up report information for tracking.

Once we came up with the ingredients for the show form, we put them together and came up with a long version of the lead tracking form shown in Figure 3–1 on pages 50–51.

Customize this form to fit your special needs. The important thing is to use the form completely. The few minutes it takes to fill out this form will not only answer many questions, but, in the long run, it will save you and your staff valuable time.

You can see on the form how we designed it for easy tracking. All follow-ups are written and dated. Before a lead is sent to a field rep, we photocopy it for our tickler files. That way we can track each lead individually and check up on progress. The nuts and bolts of postshow follow-up will be discussed in more detail in Chapter 8.

An old, but classic story concerns an exhibitor who went to a trade show with the objective of collecting leads. Every day at the end of the show he carefully secured the day's leads in a locked cabinet. At the following year's show, the same cabinet was set up at the back of the booth and unlocked. You guessed it, the leads from the previous year were still secure. As I stated, it's an old story, but certainly one to keep in mind. Remember—it doesn't matter how many leads you get, if you don't do anything with them. Design a lead tracking form, then use it!

Training

Of course, all this planning doesn't benefit anyone if the people involved don't know what's going on. Both the exhibit staff and field reps need to be trained and educated on how to maximize their effectiveness before, during, and after the trade show. It's just as important for them to understand the *why* as it is for them to understand the *what*. If you want your exhibit and field staff to support your show efforts enthusiastically, you'll want to do the same.

Figure 3–1   Show Lead Form

(Front of form)

Trade Show _____

Rep Name _____

Date _____

1   2   3

Contact Name _____

Company Name _____

Address _____

City, State _____ Zip _____

Telephone _____

Fax _____

Company Profile _____

_____

_____

Product Interest

    A _____

    B _____

    C _____

    D _____

Area of Use _____

_____

Budget _____

Buying Time Frame _____

_____

Other Buying Influences

    Name _____

    Title _____

    Name _____

    Title _____

(Back of form)

Requests Personal Call _____ Date _____
Requests Literature _____
Requests Samples _____ Date _____
   Which Ones _____
Comments from Prospect _____
_____
_____

Personal Comment about Prospect _____
_____
_____

Recorded by _____
_____ Mailed Literature on _____
_____ Date _____
_____ Follow-up Telephone Call on _____
_____ Date _____
Turned Over to Salesperson _____
Follow-up Reports
Date _____

Date _____

Date _____

Date _____

Most people think of trade show training as just boothmanship. It's more than that. Boothmanship only covers the actual
floor selling process, not preshow or postshow efforts. I've established the importance of preshow and postshow planning and
marketing, so it stands to reason that any training and education
should address those areas.

Preshow Training and Education

Make sure everyone understands what the company expects from the trade show and what his or her individual responsibility is. Then elaborate on how to accomplish show objectives.

Make sure that everybody involved in the trade show understands corporate objectives. During the period of two months to twelve months before the show, send everybody a monthly status report. From two months on in, send reports out every week. They can be short, even one page; the point is to make team members feel they are an important part of the planning process. They then become an integral part of the show's success.

Another preshow sales tactic is to call targeted prospects for preshow contact; sales reps can often provide a list of past and potential buyers. Hold weekly pep rallies to encourage your staff members to get on the phone and make show appointments. Prizes awarded for confirmed appointments add to the hype. Incentives are an important tool for motivating the inside staff and the reps. If your staff needs training in telephone skills, there are a number of excellent telemarketing programs available. If you have a large budget, hire an outside consultant to put on a customized training session. If you happen to know of one in your area, great. If not, I highly recommend George Walther, author of the top selling book *Phone Power*. George is one of the premier telemarketing consultants in the world, and, in my opinion, one of the best speakers and trainers. If you don't have the budget to bring George in personally, he has a complete line of audio and video albums. Here's how to contact George:

George Walther
401 Second Avenue South
Suite 700
Seattle, WA 98104
206/340-1200

(Be sure to say I told you to call. I don't get any commission off this recommendation, but maybe he'll give you a good deal.)

During the Show or Boothmanship Training

Most companies make the mistake of assuming there is little difference between normal field sales and trade show sales. As a result, they don't see a need for any special training for themselves or their booth staff. Unfortunately for them, there is a vast difference between field sales and trade show sales.

In field sales you go to the client, in trade show sales the client comes to you. Typically, when a sales rep makes a call on a client or prospect, the rep must go to the client's office. Not only is this time consuming, but there is a certain loss of control of the situation; this doesn't happen at a trade show. Where else can you go and have potential buyers just wander into your arms?

In the field, you are on their turf. In a trade show, they are on yours. When you call on a prospect, a certain amount of intimidation arises from being on someone else's turf. You aren't familiar with the surroundings. They can make you wait in the lobby, see drop in visitors, and take phone calls. It can be very uncomfortable. At a trade show, you control the environment of your booth. Yes, there are distractions; a trade show can be very noisy. But you can set up your booth any way you want. You can design it to look like your office, the great outdoors, or even your production line. Because you control the environment, to a certain extent you control the prospects.

In the field it's just you and the buyer. At a trade show, it's you and everybody else. Trade shows are like shopping malls. Prospects can come into your booth and listen to your sales pitch, then walk to your competition's booth to compare products. They discover almost immediately whether your products stack up against the competition. Are you as good, better, worse, cheaper, more expensive, longer lasting, more reliable, or guaranteed? When you're in their office, it's easier to claim your product is superior. At a trade show, you've got to be able to stand behind your claims, because they can be tested immediately. It's imperative that you know exactly what you're talking about.

In the field, it's not always possible to demonstrate your product; a trade show is perfect for demonstrations. If you sell heavy equipment, such as telephone interconnect systems, mainframe computers, or aircraft engines, it's just not possible to bring your product to the customer for an on-site demonstration. Conversely, a trade show is perfect for demonstrations. You can give a hands-on demonstration of your new time-management software; you can put cross sections of products on display for easy inspection; even custom demonstrations can be arranged to show your products in their best light.

In the field you can't be in two places at once. At a trade show, it's possible for you to demonstrate and sell your product to more than one prospect at a time. Studies have shown that, on average, you will see more customers and prospects in three days at a show than you'll see in six months in the field.[3]

According to the McGraw-Hill Research Lab, closing an initial sale in the field takes an average of 5.5 calls. By initiating the contact at a trade show, it only takes an average of 1.8 calls.[4]

Trade show selling takes us out of our comfort zone. Any type of selling is uncomfortable, but in degrees, trade show selling is among the most difficult. It's only natural for people to spend time with people they like and know. Sales reps are no different. They spend more time and make more sales calls on old clients, customers, and even prospects. It's hard to get salespeople to make cold calls or to follow up on leads we send them. For the same reason, it's uncomfortable to work trade shows. The booth staff sees more new faces in three of four days of a trade show than they see all year in the field.

Through boothmanship training, a sales staff learns the differences between field sales and trade show sales; they learn how to utilize such differences to their advantage. They learn how to approach prospects and qualify them quickly. They learn how to efficiently, effectively, and professionally work a trade show to help your business reach its objectives.

Some Alternatives

All this planning is great if everything from your end fits. By that I mean your company supports all your extensive and expensive plans, your budget is approved, and you have enough people to staff the booth efficiently and effectively. Unfortunately, for a lot of us, that's a pipe dream. Trade shows are expensive. Even if you

---

[3]According to William Mee, president of the Trade Show Bureau.
[4]McGraw-Hill Lab of Advertising Performance (1985). Specific source is the "Trade Show Bureau Research Report No. 2020," July 1986.

were only to rent a ten-foot space and run the show yourself, expenses could reach several thousand dollars.

Maybe you're not in a position to spend that kind of money at a trade show just yet. Maybe you only want to check out the show for possible future participation. Maybe the show is so popular that you can't get a space. Maybe you don't feel the show warrants spending a lot of money on a booth.

Working a trade show doesn't have to be a black and white issue of whether you exhibit or not. Just because you've decided not to exhibit at a particular show doesn't mean you can't take advantage of it. After all, many of your major buyers will all be in one location for several days. Work the show anyway, even if you don't rent space. Although many companies claim to do this, they really aren't any different from the company that puts up a booth and waits for customers to flock because they don't plan ahead. They don't set show objectives or make appointments with customers and prospects. They just go to the show and walk around. In doing this, they miss the many ways to take advantage of a show.

Make It a Big Sales Call

When you go see a current customer or new prospect, you have to make an appointment. If you know that several of your clients or prospects will be attending a particular trade show, call them. Explain that your company won't be exhibiting at the show, but you plan to be in town to attend. Suggest getting together for a short meeting. Unless you call the day before the show and the prospect's time is all booked, he or she will say yes. After all, he is attending the show to meet with people like you. Just because you don't have a booth doesn't mean you can't meet with clients and prospects.

Benefits of This Strategy

Daily flexibility. If you don't have an exhibit, you're not tied to particular space. Because you don't have to be at an exhibit when the show opens, you can have a leisurely breakfast with a client. You can eat lunch at any time (many show staffers can't even take lunch) and leave the show at any time. Many attendees want to avoid the mad rush to the buses and taxis, so they'll leave early. Join them.

Movability. You can literally be a portable exhibit. Some shows are so big that buyers have to set up appointments in geographical clusters. A buyer may want to see you, but the only time available is Thursday morning at 10:15, when he's in the South Arena. No problem exists because you aren't tied down.

Time management. You don't have to be out of touch with your office. Often it's difficult for show staff to contact the home office and take care of other business. You don't have that problem because you organize your own day. So, not only can you contact the office and reach customers by phone when you have to, but you can do it away from the noise of the show. Show-related appointments and other daily business duties don't have to clash.

Entertainment and hospitality. If you require a place to meet with prospects, then spend a few hundred dollars and get a suite. If your suite is convenient to the show site, people will come when invited. You can even set up a display in the room if you have to. (I discuss hospitality suites in more detail in Chapter 7.)

Less stress. You won't have to set up a booth or tear it down, which also saves you from working with unions. You don't have to stay in a booth all day culling through strangers to find qualified buyers, so there's no need to stand all day and worry about proper body language.

Less cost. An obvious reason, but an important factor to consider. You avoid the cost of the booth space, exhibit and graphics, freight, services, and advertising. You also save money on travel expenses, because you can fly in as late as the day before the show begins and leave even before the show is over.

Check out the trends and competition. When you're not having appointments, be sure to spend time walking the show. Visit your competition and see what's new. Also see who's visiting their booth; you might pick up some new leads. Be sure to cover the whole show. Many of the newest products are brought out by small companies relegated to little ten-foot exhibits on the outside aisles or downstairs. Keep your eyes and ears open.

Work the show floor. When walking through a show, I'm as conscious of the badges of people walking by me as I am of the booths. Many times I've run into prospects who, for one reason or another, weren't able to come by my booth. Because you don't have an exhibit, it's doubly important for you to be aware of people around you. Look for possible contacts on the bus, in the cafeteria, in your competition's booth, at the shoeshine stand. I've even met people in the men's room. Keep your eyes and ears open.

Seminars and workshops. By not having an exhibit, you have the flexibility of adjusting your schedule to attend speeches and programs. This is important to your continuing education in your field. Furthermore, these sessions are heavily attended by buyers.

A bonus reason. Something magical happens on the last day of the show. Usually a short day, it becomes a big indoor swap meet. I've seen people pushing shopping carts up and down aisles to buy samples at rock bottom prices. Who needs it? And because you don't have an exhibit, you don't have to stay!

Don't misinterpret me. I'm not saying that these practices are superior to having a booth at the show. But if after careful analysis, you decide not to exhibit, then consider working the show this way. In many ways, it's just as exhausting as having a booth, but for less cost, it might also be just as rewarding.

CHAPTER 4

Preshow Marketing

The Trade Show Rule

The trade show management promised you more attendees than the entire population of Tokyo. On the afternoon of the first day, however, you find it possible to shoot a cannon down the aisles. And of shows that have an attendance of 100,000-plus, you can assume that only 20,000–30,000 of the attendees are legitimate buyers, if you're lucky. That means that only 25 percent of the people walking into your booth are real buyers.

Let's do a little simple math on that last example. If the show is open for a total of thirty hours over four days, you should be able to average six contacts per hour. That's 180 total contacts. Figuring that 25 percent of them are legitimate buyers, that's only forty-five real contacts. If I said that you were going to a show with 100,000 attendees and would come away with only forty-five leads, would you think I was crazy? Would you even go? Yet, that is what normally happens to most businesses at trade shows.

This brings us to what I call *The Trade Show Rule:*

> The ultimate success of your trade show lies entirely with you and has nothing, repeat, nothing to do with show management.

Of course, right now you're shaking your head and quietly saying to yourself, "This guy's crazy. The management of *our* trade shows is very much involved in bringing buyers in. Why, I just saw a large ad in our industry's trade magazine inviting buyers to the show."

That may be true. But before you close this book and donate it to Goodwill, let's discuss exactly what you can expect from trade show management.

Trade Show Management

Trade show managers are running a business. They have a product, the trade show, and the measure of success for them is how many square feet of floor space they sell. The more floor space they sell, the more successful they are. And the way they insure that the show will be held again next year is to have happy exhibitors. Somewhere along the line, someone decided that the number of people attending a trade show determined its success, and the exhibitors went along with this. After all, if 25,000 buyers attend a show and you don't get any sales, it must be your fault. So, the bigger the attendance, the happier the exhibitors. The happier the exhibitors, the more successful the show. The more successful the show, the faster the companies sign up for next year. And the beat goes on.

The catch is that sheer attendance has nothing to do with success at a trade show. Your success is unique to your company and may be based on many factors: sales, new prospects, developing relationships with customers, product testing, and market research, to name a few. I seriously doubt that you define 25,000 attendees as an objective.

The preshow marketing help you can expect from show management includes promoting the event through direct mail, trade magazine ads, and ticket promotions (sometimes). These marketing efforts are aimed at a broad audience in order to attract large numbers of attendees. Somewhere within that large group of attendees should be your target market, but it is up to you to attract the right people to your booth. Remember, show management guarantees attendance, not buyers.

Preshow Marketing

Preshow marketing can determine your success or failure at the show. The primary reason behind this assertion is also the most obvious; if your target customers don't know you're going to be at the trade show, how can they be expected to look for your booth? Do you really believe that you can just rent booth space, put your exhibit up, and wait for the crowds? In a study for the Trade Show Bureau, six factors were identified as influencing a prospect's decision to visit a selected exhibit.[1]

1. Interesting product demonstrations: 28 percent. An attendee is attracted by top quality, professionally handled demonstrations. This doesn't necessarily mean using professional models, actors, or actresses, either. It simply means that demonstrations were being presented in an interesting and appealing fashion.
2. Exhibit location: 23 percent. Obviously, it's much better to be as close to the front and center of the exhibition hall as possible.

    Even though this appears to contradict what I wrote in Chapter 3 on booth location, it doesn't. The first reference is to booth traffic throughout the show. Location should not affect traffic. This study refers to the reason why an attendee visited a specific exhibit. Although buyers do, in fact, walk through an entire show, it is unlikely they visit a specific company against the back wall on a lower level because of the location.
3. Associate recommendation: 22 percent. One of the most powerful means of getting people to come to your booth is by having your customers and professional contacts arrange for prospects to visit.
4. Exhibit presentation: 13 percent. The three things an attendee sees first are the exhibit, the products, and the personnel. These three factors work together to form your exhibit's presentation. Make sure they're good.
5. Sales rep recommendation: 12 percent. Salespeople know the names and addresses of their target market and can extend personal invitations to its members. The prospects then know what you'll be displaying and where you'll be located.
6. Exhibit size: 1 percent. The sheer size of an exhibit is enough to create curiosity for a booth.

[1] "Trade Show Bureau Research Report No. 13," July 1982.

Of these six factors, the study shows that there are many influ-ences over which an exhibitor has direct control. This is signifi-cant in that utilizing the most controllable reasons in a collective effort can boost the effectiveness of the show measurably.

Other than the obvious reason of getting people into your booth at a trade show, there is one more compelling reason for using preshow marketing. It helps stretch out the show. Typi-cally, a company treats a trade show as a two- to five-day event, depending on its length, with the focus almost entirely on mak-ing those few days as productive as possible. This approach uti-lizes only one-third of a show's potential marketing power. A trade show is actually utilized at its fullest in a four- to five-month campaign, with the show situated in the middle. A trade show has three definite time frames—before, during, and after. Each of those has its own unique marketing forte. By effectively tying your marketing campaign in with the upcoming show two to three months before its opening, you can create enthusiasm and anticipation for the event, emphasizing exciting and new products and services you'll be offering. This not only generates interest in your customers and prospects, but in your employees as well. Then, by working an exciting show followed by a slam-bang postshow campaign, the synergistic result will most cer-tainly be successful. A strong preshow marketing campaign ensures the success of a show *before* the show opens.

Several different methods can be utilized in a preshow cam-paign. How to implement some of these methods encompasses the remainder of this chapter.

Personal Invitations

By far the most effective way to reach potential attendees is through personal invitations. The first step in this process is to identify your target audience and assemble a mailing list; in-clude current customers and prospects. Assembling the current customer list is easy, but it will probably require extensive work to gather a prospect list. Several ways exist to gather these names and addresses. Your sales reps should know the names of several prospects they haven't been able to sell, yet. You can also get mailing lists through reputable list brokers, a specific trade or professional association, a trade publication, even from the trade show itself. Be sure to ask only for the list segments most applicable to your target audience.

Once you've compiled these lists, start using them two to three months prior to the show. Begin with a personal invitation from the most prestigious person in the department (how about your company president?). Don't make the letter too long; just briefly tell them the name of the show, its dates, what products you'll be showing, why it would benefit them to visit you, where you will be located, and the name, address, and telephone number of someone to contact for more information. The important thing about personal invitations is that they are personal. The prospect feels cared for as an individual. Don't, therefore, send your invitations via bulk mail and don't stuff them full of product sheets and pricing information. Save that for the show.

One week after this initial letter, the contact person should follow up with personal phone calls, letters, and invitations to persuade the prospect to visit your booth. Don't be satisfied with a mere confirmation that they'll visit the booth. Get even more personal and ask for an appointment. There are two very good reasons for doing this. First is commitment; they have an obligation to show up since they set an appointment. And second, the salesperson responsible for that prospect can arrange to be in the booth for that appointment. Such appointments are key to trade show success. If every salesperson books an average of four appointments per hour, then the show radiates success even before it opens. Primary goals are already accomplished; if anybody else comes into the booth it's merely a perk.

The personal invitation doesn't work all the time. Sometimes you have to be a little more creative to get your prospect's attention (as shown in the example on page 64).

There is another method I've used several times when inviting specific people to my exhibits. I first utilized it after trying, with no success, to make a trade show appointment with the president of a *Fortune* 500 corporation. Although I didn't have a problem getting him on the phone, he maintained that his show schedule was already packed and he couldn't possibly see me; he just didn't have the time. I was waiting for a flight from Los

A small Southern California toy company planned to exhibit at the New York Premium/Incentive Show. In researching the show they discovered there were going to be more than 30,000 attendees. The sales manager was excited until he found out there would also be 1,500 other exhibitors. An added concern was the knowledge that Apple Computer would be across the aisle from them with a 1,200-square-foot exhibit. The toy company feared its 100-square-foot booth would be dwarfed by the computer giant.

To get the attention of its prospects, the toy company put together a wave campaign to personally invite its target market and set up appointments. A wave campaign is a short-term series of coordinated marketing steps taken to accomplish a particular objective. In this case, the campaign was a three-stage mailing with each letter designed to generate interest in the next. Ten weeks prior to the show, the first letter—sent from the president—invited all prospects to visit them at the show. The second letter included a floor plan with the company's location clearly marked in red.

In the third mailing, knowing the attendees would be on their feet for four days, and that all that walking and standing would make for tired, sore feet, the sales manager sent a pair of Dr. Scholl's footpads—with his corporate logo silkscreened right on the pad. If the prospects used the pad, every time they put their shoes on or took them off, they would see the toy company's logo. Follow-up phone calls two weeks before the show netted dozens of appointments. The amount of drop-ins at the show was also high. The result of this creative and personal campaign? More than 90 percent of the targeted prospects visited the exhibit.

Angeles to Chicago a couple of weeks prior to the show when an idea came to me. I ran over to the flight insurance counter and took out an insurance policy. I made the president of that company the beneficiary, attached a "thinking of you," note to it, and sent it to him. Two days later, after I returned from Chicago, he set the appointment. (Maybe he didn't want *me* to show up for the appointment.)

Telemarketing

So you don't have a big advertising budget. That's okay, it isn't necessary to spend a fortune to have an effective advertising campaign before a trade show because there are several different types of advertising available. Remember, as you plan, think "collective advertising" and spread your ad dollars over more than one vehicle.

Telemarketing is the next best thing to personal invitations. If you currently use telemarketing in your marketing mix, then it will be easy to implement it in your preshow marketing plan. Simply compile a list of your target market and have your telemarketing staff phone for appointments six weeks prior to the show's opening.

If you do not use telemarketing in your business, you may be getting left behind. I strongly encourage you to learn about it through books, tapes, and seminars. A simple beginning, however, would be to compile your list of target prospects, then write a very simple script. Here is an example:

Hello, may I speak with Mr./Mrs./Ms. _____ ?

Good morning/afternoon Mr./Mrs./Ms. _____ .

This is _____ . I am calling for the Widget Manufacturing Company in Seattle. How are you?

(Pause)

Are you planning to attend the National Premium/ Incentive Show in New York May 5–8?

(Pause)

(If no) We're sorry to hear that. We were looking forward to showing you _____ . Will there be anyone else from your company whom we might be able to see?

(If no) Thanks anyway, Mr./Mrs./Ms. _____ . I'll make sure you still receive information about the _____ . Goodbye.

(If yes to the first question) Great! We'd like very much to set up an appointment for you to visit our booth. Would Monday morning at 11:30 be all right, or would Tuesday afternoon at 2:00 be better for you?

(Pause)

(If they pick one) I've got you down to visit our exhibit on _____ . I'll put a confirmation in the mail. Thank you for your time, Mr./Mrs./Ms. _____ .

(If they don't want to set an appointment) I understand, Mr./Mrs./Ms. _____ . Can we at least set up either Monday morning or Tuesday afternoon? (I've never been turned down for this.)

(Pause)

Fine, thank you so much. I'll pass on this information to Mr./Mrs./Ms. _____ , who will be looking for you. Goodbye.

Such calls are very simple and shouldn't take more than a few minutes. If you can't spare anyone to make those calls, hire people for temporary work. Give them the list and the script. You can pay them hourly or, better yet, pay them per appointment made.

Direct Mail

Next to personal invitations and telemarketing, direct mail is the best way to reach potential attendees. Compile a list of current clients, known prospects, people who have requested product information in the last twelve months, and other likely sources. Again, you can add to the number of names by purchasing a list from a reputable broker, business association, or trade publication.

Follow the same plan as that designed for personal invitations; but instead of personal follow-ups, send two or three mailings beginning three months before the show, spaced three to four weeks apart. Include a small premium or incentive to encourage them to visit your exhibit. There are literally thousands of ideas available, so don't just fall back on the standard pencil, calendar, or keychain. Get out your local yellow pages and look up "Advertising Specialties" for a distributor near you; then go visit the showroom and explain your objective and budget. The distributor should have plenty of samples and catalogs for you to choose from. This is a specialized industry; let the distributor help you.

If you do plan to use a premium or incentive, be sure to give the advertising specialty distributor plenty of time (four to six weeks) to get the products for you. Also, expect to put a 50 percent deposit down on your order. Unless they've been working with you for some time, you probably won't get away from this.

Use your imagination when designing this series of mailings; obviously, the bigger your budget, the more options you have. A professionally produced audio tape inviting the prospect to visit you is a great idea. It's common practice for people to throw away junk mail before it's even read (especially if it's bulk mail), but I've never heard of anyone throwing away an audio tape received in the mail.

Maybe you don't have a budget that will cover audio tapes, yet need something eye-catching. When you run your series of ads in the trade publication (remember, the Wheeler study referred to in Chapter 2 encouraged a collective effort of promotion), ask the publisher to run off an extra thousand copies of the page with your ad. It's inexpensive and you'll then be able to incorporate the ad in your direct mail campaign, including a note stating, "As seen in *Widget Trade News.*"

Trade Publications

Trade publications are a good way to reach your target market; however, steer clear of show issues, especially if your ad budget is small. In the advertising world, it's better to employ frequency over size; that is, it's better to run a series of smaller ads for a few months before the show than to have a full-page, four-color ad in a show issue, even if the publisher passes out thousands of bonus copies at the show. A study conducted by Exhibit Surveys for the Trade Show Bureau shows booth traffic increases by about 40 percent for every four pages of preshow advertising.[2] It's my opinion that the show issue doesn't get read until after the show, if at all. Attendees at a show don't arrive, pick up show issues, and then sit down to read them before visiting booths. They set their schedule before walking into the arena. Be a part of their schedule by utilizing trade publications early and frequently.

Advertising Specialties

Advertising specialties are the little giveaway items you see at every trade show, for which there are literally thousands of possible ideas. They can be one of the most powerful methods for creating brand awareness and name retention. At the same time, they are probably one of the most misunderstood and misused marketing tools available. The Advertising Specialty Institute (ASI) was founded to help bring some semblance of order to a very confusing industry.

[2]"Trade Show Bureau Research Report No. 27," October 1985.

An item must meet three qualifications with regard to function, printed message, and price before it is defined as an advertising specialty.

Function

Those plastic bags given out by the millions at trade shows are a good example of an advertising specialty product. Their function is to hold things. They hold flyers, brochures, and other small giveaways. The problem with these bags is that they don't have a long life span. As soon as the stuff inside the bag is sorted through, the bag is tossed out. I don't recommend plastic bags.

Imprinted with a Logo or Message

Every advertising specialty product will have a corporate logo or advertising message imprinted somewhere on its surface. Ways to imprint include silk screening, engraving, hot stamping, and printing.

Reasonable Cost

An advertising specialty product is usually fairly inexpensive. It's not unusual for one to cost just a few pennies. If you are planning to give every attendee walking by your booth a gift and there are 65,000 attendees, you don't want to spend very much. If, however, you're planning to give a nice gift to your top 100 customers at the show, you might want to spend a little more.

Reasons for Using a Giveaway

You might ask why you should use a giveaway. Although I'm not necessarily endorsing the use of advertising specialty products, I do feel there is a place for them in a marketing mix. And, quite possibly, the trade show is a good place for them. If you elect to use giveaways, select something that will stand out in the crowd, something that will help your prospect think of you.

Personalize it. Besides having your corporate logo on it, engrave the recipient's name on it. It adds a special personal touch; also, people rarely throw out something imprinted with their name.

Ensure high perceived value. One company used Swiss Army knives as part of an elaborate giveaway in a promotional campaign aimed at presidents of companies that purchased heavy equipment. Although compared to a truck costing hundreds of thousands of dollars, a Swiss Army knife is inexpensive, the perceived value was high and the giveaway was a success because of the first-class campaign.

Build in exclusivity by limiting distribution. My wife works for Walker Manufacturing Company, a division of Tenneco. The company manufactures mufflers and catalytic converters. Like other automotive aftermarket companies, Walker uses several giveaway items—T-shirts, hats, knives, coffee cups, and jackets to name a few. They also use a special black jacket that everybody wants. Not everybody has it, however, because only a limited supply exists; it's become a special prize, a semi-status symbol among customers.

Cloak it in celebrity status. After Jack Nicklaus won the Masters with an oversized putter, a sales bonanza started for that particular brand. Everybody likes to have a product with such status behind it. If you can create status, capitalize on its value.

Provide a name-brand product or something designed by a renowned person. Imagine giving away copies of a Leroy Neiman specially painted for a customer's company. It would be even more successful if Neiman did the painting at the show.

Make it fit the taste, position, and status of the receiver. Some companies keep using little stick-on fuzzy birds at trade shows to promote their name. The problem comes when they stick one on a CEO's $1,000 Georgio Armani suit. Be careful and be sensitive to the receiver.

Flatter the receiver. Create subtle pats on the back that keep silently applauding and patting for years, and, of course, are seen by the right people. As an example: I have a paperweight in the shape of a star. I did a favor for a client and received it with my name engraved. It's proudly displayed on my desk for everybody to see. I've also seen companies use specially designed pens with the corporate logo imprinted as "medals of honor" for their salespeople. When somebody pulls out the special pen to write up an order, customers automatically know this salesperson is a winner.

Add a twist. At one medical trade show, a company offered free teddy bears to every pediatrician invited to view a sales presentation. More than 93 percent of the invitees responded. Can you imagine a huge line of doctors waiting to get their teddy bears?

Select a usable, functional item. Functionality gives the receiver a reason for keeping your gift handy. It works, and that's its reason for being. It doesn't exist solely for self-aggrandizement. I use a pocket shoe polisher as a giveaway. Because I stress the importance of well-shined shoes at trade shows, this is a natural for me. It is very functional and people really like it. In fact, it's so well-liked that I get calls for replacements!

Present the gift politely. Forcing a gift on someone defeats its purpose. Respect your attendees, even if they refuse your trinket.

Not one of these ten tips is the ultimate answer for every problem. But the more of them that can logically be built into the marketing tool used, the better the probability that it will be kept. And that's the name of the game.

Local Newspapers and Cable TV

Many companies run ads in the business sections of local newspapers a day or two before the show opens. Be very careful to determine that this is a good idea before you commit to it, however. Trade show visitors travel greater distances than most companies think. A survey of regional and national shows revealed that 64 percent of all visitors traveled more than 200 miles to the show.

More and more large trade shows are broadcasting reports in convention hotels via cable TV. They often offer advertising at a fairly reasonable cost. Unfortunately they probably broadcast to a bunch of empty rooms. If people are in town to attend the show, why would they be in their hotel room?

Types of Advertising to Consider

There are many other ways to advertise your presence at an upcoming trade show, and you may certainly consider them as possibilities in your ad campaign. However, *caveat emptor*, buyer beware! For one reason or another, most of these methods usually aren't recommended.

Billboards

At large national and international shows some companies use billboards to advertise booth location. Unfortunately, there isn't any way to quantify a return on this investment. It is simply brand-awareness advertising. Also, a billboard reaches everybody who drives by, not just your target market. Don't put your money into billboards, no matter how big you are. There are many more quantifiable ways of using your trade show promotion dollar.

City Show Guides

These are specialized visitor's guides distributed at trade shows; basically, they provide information on where to go and what to do in the convention city. The main problem with these is the same as with the trade publication's show issue. It's passed out during the show. Too late! Remember, you want the prospects to have you on their appointment calendar before they arrive at the show.

Wraparounds

Some magazines and newspapers will put an information piece designed to look like their cover around an issue (hence, wraparound). Because most attendees stay at one or two hotels, you can arrange for special delivery of these to attendees' rooms. This is a very eye-catching and tactical promotion, although there are three drawbacks. First, all the attendees at these hotels, whether they are your prospects or not, will get an issue. Second, it happens at the show—probably too late. Last, it can be very expensive.

There is a way to offset the first two drawbacks of this and some magazine publishers will comply with you on it. Have the wraparound designed several months in advance, then send the publisher the names and addresses of your target list. He or she then sends your "special issue" out with the regular mailing.

Stuffers

A must. Design and print an inexpensive flyer announcing the show, its dates, your location, and what you'll be displaying. Then starting three months before the show, include it in every piece of mail (invoices, statements) that leaves your company.

Publicity and Promotion

These are very powerful and often overlooked tools. Most small businesses don't even try to get publicity, when it is actually quite simple. You can do it yourself, too.

Newsletters

If you have a newsletter, this is a great way to announce your trade show participation. Your customers and prospects are already expecting it. Prominently display the announcement and be sure to include the name and telephone number of a knowledgeable contact in your company.

Press Releases

The purpose of a press release is to communicate newsworthy information effectively. The contents vary. They may encompass a new product, an improvement on an existing product, an industry breakthrough, new applications for current products, and personnel changes. The key thing to remember about a press release is that it is not supposed to be an advertisement. Write it like a news story. Give all the pertinent information—who, what, where, when, why, and how—in the first paragraph. Then detail all other features and benefits.

A good press release is one page long, double spaced; it's short. At the top of the page, type *For Immediate Release,* or *For Release on* _____ (whatever date is applicable). Then write the headline and story. At the bottom of the page, type *For further information, contact:* _____ and provide your name, address, and phone number. An editor may want to contact you for more information in order to write an in-depth story. If a photo is available and applicable, include a sharp five-by-seven black-and-white print.

Send the release to all magazine publications at least three to four months prior to when you want it published. That's how far ahead magazines work on editorial content. Newspapers work on a much shorter time frame. Just a couple of weeks notice should be sufficient for them.

Not all publications will use your releases. But if you get one or two printed, it's worth it.

Trade Publications

If you are an advertiser or potential advertiser, magazines will often write about your company, your products, and you. Although this practice is not recorded in any publishers' corporate policy statements, and many of them would vehemently deny it, the fact is, publishers stay in business by keeping their clients happy. A publisher can provide additional publicity at no cost to the advertiser. The magazine is going to have editorial pages, anyway; they might as well be used to promote advertisers (and their egos). Go ahead and ask for free publicity. Ask for it just before you sign the contract. The worst they can say is no; but the odds are you will receive some very good articles.

If you're not an advertiser, or if you run into one of those magazines whose salespeople don't talk with editorial people, you can still get publicity. Give a magazine a good reason to run your story. When talking to an editor, look for an angle that will appeal to the magazine's readership. Don't just suggest they write about you. Offer some unique information about your trade. Editors aren't in the business of giving away free publicity; they're in the information dissemination business: New trends. New break-throughs. What's happening in the industry. Give them some-thing to write about and they'll do so.

Sometimes an editor will tell you what type of story he's look-ing for. He knows the audience. Give him a story he'll be eager to print. An editor of a large trade publication told me that 80 per-cent of his ideas for stories come from outside sources. Help make his job easier and get some publicity in the process.

Trade Show Seminars

I'm not talking about attending them. I'm talking about *giving* them. Surveys have shown that one of the strongest attractions of trade shows are the educational sessions. By participating in these, you are not only exposed to more prospects, but they see you as an expert.

Think about what knowledge you have that might be useful to the attendees. Then contact the show management and offer your services as a speaker. Ask what types of programs they look for or what the theme of the upcoming show is. You can then custom design a program for them or offer yourself for specific panel discussions. Be sure to do this nine to twelve months in ad-vance of the show, since that's usually how far in advance they plan.

Although it's not always easy to be placed on the program list, it is possible. And once you've been selected, publicity follows. Not only are you able to capitalize on your presentation by pro-moting it through your own direct mail campaign, but the show will promote it too. And, of course, your friendly, neighborhood trade publication should also be interested in doing a follow-up story about the "expert."

Be Creative

It's important to remember that all preshow marketing plans should be designed with your specific show objectives in mind. Regardless of whether your objectives include sales, new leads, public relations, or product research, you want attendees to visit your exhibit. Be creative in your tactics. The following are some ideas to stimulate your creative juices.

Show Badges

If the show has preregistration through the mail, why not offer to handle registration for your customers and prospects? Arrange for all the badges and then mail them to customers and prospects with an invitation to visit your booth. You can drop a subtle, "Hey, look what we did for you, now you can do this for us." They'll stop by.

Arrange for a Block of Hotel Rooms

A client of mine in Las Vegas has been doing this for years during the Winter Consumer Electronics Show. Each year he sets aside a block of fifty rooms at one of the major hotels. He then offers these rooms as well as airport pickup service to top customers. The customer still pays for the room, but doesn't have to hassle with reservations or taxis. Some customers even joke that they do business with my client just so they will have a room in Las Vegas each year! (An additional benefit from this is knowing where your top customers are staying during the show.)

Trade Show Appointment Books

Put together a pocket planner for prospects to use for scheduling appointments during the show. Send it to them about four to six weeks before the show. Be sneaky and fill in one of the time slots for a visit to your booth; they'll get a kick out of it and be there at the appointed time. If they can't make the appointment, they usually call to arrange another time. This planner can also be a great way to promote your products or services through photos and "ads."

Hold a Golf Tournament the Day before the Show

It's not unusual for attendees to mix a little pleasure with business, especially if the show site is a nice one. One company I know in Southern California arranges a round of golf the day before the show opens at one of the top local courses. They turn it into a small tournament, and bring in a PGA tour player to mingle with the guests. The customers and prospects pay their own way for one extra day and have the time of their lives. Very little business is handled on the course, but every one of those attendees makes an appointment to visit the exhibit during the show.

Trade a Book for an Appointment

Have you written a book? One author I know, whose company exhibits at a lot of shows, offers an autographed copy of his book to everyone who visits the exhibit. People walk away with something they'll keep, and he walks away with a lot of leads.

Summary

Let's face it. Preshow marketing is important. The sad thing is that most companies do very little. Remember the Trade Show Rule. Plan an effective preshow campaign that will draw hundreds of qualified buyers to your exhibit. I say *effective,* because many of the companies who say they use preshow marketing really don't. Sending out those preprinted registration flyers from show management is not effective. Telling buyers, in casual conversation, to "drop by sometime during the show" is not effective. Sending a memo to all your reps two weeks before the show imploring them to bring their key prospects by the booth is not effective.

Those companies that understand they are responsible for the success of their show make a dedicated commitment to effective preshow marketing. This commitment ensures their success.

Let me tell you a short story. A chicken and a pig decided to take a walk through town one beautiful spring day. As they were strolling by a small cafe, they happened to notice a sign in the window.

Two Eggs — $ .65
Slice of Ham — $1.00

The chicken was outraged. Squawking and flapping about, the chicken turned to the pig and huffed, "I can't believe it! I can't believe it! Two...TWO eggs are only sixty-five cents and one measly slice of ham is a whole dollar!"

The pig calmly looked at the sign, turned to the chicken and said, "Well, the way I see it is this—the two eggs are a service, but the slice of ham is a total commitment!"

A well-planned, well-designed, and well-executed preshow marketing campaign takes a total, dedicated commitment. But in the end, you will find the time and effort are well spent.

CHAPTER 5

At the Show

Preshow Planning

Effective preshow planning and marketing need to be reinforced by a solid foundation of effort at the show. Last-minute problems do occur, but there are a number of things to help alleviate them.

When to Arrive

The show opens on Thursday. To save money, the show staff flies in on Wednesday night. They plan to set up early Thursday morning. Although this is a very common practice, it is very risky. Major problems can occur.

Trade shows are highly stressful situations. It's been rumored that Murphy's Law was named after an ex-exhibit manager. Believe me—if something can go wrong, it will. Exhibits don't arrive on time. Products are missing. Literature gets sent to the wrong place. The labor you ordered never shows up. The carpet is the wrong color. Another company is in your booth (it's happened to me). Your flights are delayed, or worse, cancelled. The show doesn't have much of a chance of success if you, your people, or your equipment isn't there on time, or at all. If any of these situations arise and you don't have the time to correct them—well, you're out of luck. The show will go on without you.

That's why I recommend arriving no later than two days before the show begins. Always have your booth ready twenty-four hours prior to the show's opening. There are two major reasons for these recommendations. First, the exhibit will be ready! After all, isn't that what you're going to the show for in the first place? By setting up the day before, you give yourself enough time to handle last-minute, unexpected emergencies. Second, you then have plenty of time to go through last-minute strategies and meetings.

In addition, if your exhibit requires outside help in being set up, be sure to coordinate this with your transportation people and show labor. Know when the exhibit is going to arrive at the show site and then plan to set up as soon as possible. By arranging to do this with the labor service ahead of time, you'll avoid potential headaches and conflicts. The best situation is to have your booth delivered and erected on the first day the show site is available.

Such forethought assures that you will be ready for the show. By having your exhibit ready twenty-four hours ahead of time, you'll be able to prepare mentally for the upcoming carnival. Trade shows are mentally and physically exhausting. So get a good night's sleep the night before the show. You'll feel fresher, less stressed out, and more alert.

When to Order Services

Even if it doesn't seem fair that you have to send your money in far ahead of time to get a discount on services, do it anyway. Your main concern should be getting the job done right, and on time. If you wait until you arrive at the show site, arranging services can take a long time. You have to stand in several different lines to order the various services you require. Then you have to wait in your booth for the services or rentals to arrive. Often, you sit in your booth and wait...and wait...and wait; sometimes these things take hours. Do you really need to go through all that?

Another benefit of preordering is that the service companies can efficiently plan on providing you with that service. By giving them advance notice, the odds are you'll arrive at the show and find your electricity, telephone, carpet, and other services all ready for you. That reduces stress.

Bring Your Exhibitor Kit

There may be some rules and regulations that affect your booth or show performance. Be sure to read them thoroughly and discuss any problems with show management. The kit will also contain the paperwork for those services you order in advance. Of course, if you've put together the *Exhibit Planning Handbook*, outlined in Chapter 3, you'll have all this.

Bring Cash, Traveler's Checks, or Credit Cards

You may have missed something in preparing for the show. If you need to get some things from show services or buy forgotten supplies from the store across the street, you'll need money. Furthermore, tips may or may not be necessary for services rendered. It's a good idea to be ready, regardless.

Installation

Do you remember the first time you attended a major national show and walked into the hall before the show opened? It probably resembled uncontrollable chaos in a concrete jungle. People were all over the place. Union laborers were puzzling over exhibit plans. Telephone installers were cherry-picking in the girders high overhead. Forklifts were speeding up and down aisles stacked with crates, cartons, and rolls of carpet. It seemed as if there were no way the show could be ready to open on time.

That's certainly the way it always seems. But somehow, magically, on the first morning of the show, everything falls into place. Forklifts and laborers fade away; carpets appear in the aisles; electricity is turned on and the hall shines. Almost miraculously, the show opens on time.

As it turns out, everybody involved in show preparation had a special job to do. Every laborer, every installer, every floor manager, every union supervisor, and every exhibit manager played an important role in getting the show ready on time.

Show preparation includes you, too. You have to make sure everything in your exhibit is in place when the doors open—

exhibit up, signage and graphics up, products out, personnel ready, crates and cartons properly stored, and booth clean. And as the old movie saying goes: You have two ways of getting all this accomplished—you can do it the hard way or you can do it the easy way.

The Hard Installation

Because you live just 100 miles away from the show site, you don't send your exhibit ahead of time; you plan to bring it in your car. You haven't ordered any services for the show, although you're going to need quite a few: electricity, a telephone, a sign for the booth, some chairs and tables (draped), a carpet, daily booth cleaning, a security cage, and a model to pass out literature. The show doesn't open until 1:00 P.M., so you plan to drive in that morning to set up, which you also plan to do yourself.

You arrive at the show site at 8:00 A.M., assuming you have plenty of time to set up. First, you need a dolly to get your booth inside because it's too large to carry—plus you have a lot of samples and literature. Hmmmm. Nobody will loan you a dolly or even a handcart; all those union guys seem to be permanently attached to one and they're not about to let go. After a frustrating hour of looking (it's 9:00) and begging ("Please, pal, I only need it for ten minutes!"), you finally relent and go to the service desk for help. You stand in line for eighteen minutes (9:18). The person behind the desk tells you to wait close by, so there you stand twiddling your thumbs. Another twenty-two minutes go by (9:40) before they locate someone with a dolly. He follows you to your car and, with your help, loads everything onto the dolly and takes it to your booth. He moves pretty fast and takes only thirty-eight more minutes of your time (10:18).

After parking your car, you go to your booth and realize you can't set up without putting the carpet down first. You hike back to the service desk and again stand in line. This time it takes only eleven minutes to get your carpet ordered and go back to your booth (10:29). You're finally settling down from the minor panic of searching for a hand cart. You figure you still have plenty of time before the show opens. To kill some time, though, you start to open some of your product and literature boxes.

Twenty minutes go by (10:49) and you're getting a little antsy because the carpet hasn't arrived yet. Another sixteen minutes pass (11:05) and you start thinking you could have ordered the electricity, telephone, chairs and tables, model, security cage, and cleaning if you had known it was going to take so long to get a lousy carpet. Finally the carpet arrives and is rolled out in one minute (11:06). You immediately begin unpacking your booth to set up. You get the framework put up when you remember you still need to order the rest of your services. You look at your watch and see that it's now 11:23. You realize you only have an hour and thirty-seven minutes before the show opens and the panic begins to set in. You race off to the service desks. Nearing them, you realize that every one of them—electricity, telephone, chairs and tables, models, security cages, and cleaning—has a separate desk. You've got to stand in every one of those lines! It's 11:26. You begin to sweat. The first line—electricity—isn't so bad. Only nine minutes gone (11:35). The next—telephone—is pretty good, too; only eight minutes (11:43). But you're getting more and more nervous, and still have four more desks to visit. There are at least ten people in line ahead of you at the furniture rental desk. The line barely crawls. Five minutes go by, then ten, fifteen, twenty! One by achingly slow one the line gets shorter. Twenty-five minutes have passed (12:08). Finally, it's your turn. You place your order, but you almost have a big payment problem. How were you supposed to know that they wouldn't bill you? Fortunately, you had your VISA card to cover it. Luckier still, they took it.

Time is really short now (12:16). You realize there is no way to get the other three services—model, security cage, and cleaning—and still have time to finish setting and cleaning up in time for the opening. You decide you don't really need cleaning, that you can do it yourself. The model is also canceled because she was only going to pass out literature anyway. And because you've never been ripped off before, you decide to hide your samples in boxes underneath the tables.

By now you're a nervous wreck. You run back to your booth and find the union supervisor waiting for you. He politely explains to you about the unwritten "Half-Hour Rule." It seems that, unless you can put up your exhibit in under thirty minutes, you must use qualified union help. He points out that you started setting up at 11:06. You turn white and start to cry; it works this time. After eliciting a promise that you'll never, ever set up or tear down your booth without union help, he lets you off the hook with a warning. It's now 12:31 P.M.

Shifting into high gear, you throw the rest of your booth together and pull out your products for display. As the magic hour of 1:00 passes, you're still setting out brochures and plugging in lights. Buyers start to roam through the aisles, but they see you're not set up and leave you alone. The chairs and table arrive at 1:30. The table drape arrives at 1:50. You still haven't cleaned up or put on a tie.

By 2:10, things in the booth are pretty much in order. Now you can go to the restroom and get dressed. But you don't have a model; if you leave your booth, it'll be unmanned. So you ask the person in the booth next door to keep an eye out. Finally, by 2:43, you're dressed and the booth looks passable. But the events of the last six hours and forty-three minutes have left you frazzled, both mentally and physically. You can't wait till the show closes at 6:00. Unfortunately, that attitude shows to everyone else, too, and carries over to the rest of the show, which is a failure.

Is this any way to work at a trade show? No, of course not. Was this scenario a farfetched fantasy—completely unrealistic? Unfortunately, no. It's surprising how many times over the years I've watched scenes from this example happen again and again.

The Easy Installation

It's 6:00 A.M. Wednesday morning and you're packing your clothes. The show is scheduled to open at 1:00 P.M. on Thursday. Because the show site is only 100 miles away, you plan to drive in. That's not a problem because you're getting an early start.

Before loading the car, you go over your trade show handbook one last time. Everything has gone smoothly and well within the time plan. The exhibit was shipped early and you've received confirmation from your carrier's local rep that it arrived at the show safely. All the products for display and literature were packed with the booth, so everything is there. You double check to see if anything is missing that you'll need: you have an exhibitor's kit, copies of all advance service orders, and enough traveler's checks to take care of any last minute items. Everything's ready, so you load the car and hit the road by 9:00.

You arrive at the show site before noon. After parking the car, you head in to your booth. The carpet you preordered is already down and everything you shipped is waiting in the booth. The preordered draped tables, chairs, electricity, security cage, and telephone connection are also in place. You have plenty of time before the labor you ordered arrives at 2:00 to set up, so you head to the service desks to confirm your model and daily cleaning.

Because you've arrived a day ahead of time, there is almost no line, and within thirty minutes you've confirmed both services. During the remaining time, you explore the show site. With your checklist in hand, you find out where the food concessions, restrooms, first aid booths, security office, fire alarms, and pay telephones are located. After finding these you head for registration to pick up your show badges and exhibitor guide. On your way back to the booth, you stop by the show office to introduce yourself to the manager.

By now it's nearly 2:00 and time to be at your booth to set up. The labor and supervisor arrive right on time. You knew they would be reliable because you hired them through an established exhibit house. They get right to work erecting the exhibit while you unpack products. It takes most of the afternoon to prepare everything to your satisfaction, but by 5:00 P.M. the booth looks great.

After storing your products in the security cage for overnight safekeeping, you head off to the hotel. You enjoy a relaxing evening and dinner, comfortable in the thought that everything is ready for tomorrow.

The morning comes. Because the show doesn't open till 1:00, you have time to take care of a number of phone calls and see one of your local clients for a short time. You arrive at the show by 11:00 to set out all your products and store the security cage behind your booth. Because of its overnight cleaning, the booth looks great.

At 12:15, the model you hired arrives and you go over her responsibilities. By 12:45, you're all set! You're fresh, excited, and anxious for the show to begin. At 1:00 P.M. the show opens and you attract the very first buyers into your booth and convert them into qualified prospects. The show becomes an unqualified success.

Does this sound like a pipe dream? Can things really run this smoothly during installation and setup? The answer is a resounding yes! By following the simple steps I've outlined on planning ahead, you will be ready to go when the show begins.

Your Products

There are three parts of a trade show that determine your success. All three are equally important. First is the booth itself. Second is the personnel staffing the booth. And third is the product or service you are selling. (Hereafter, in this section, when I refer to *product*, it means product or service.)

What your product is or what it does is not important here. But there are four matters associated with your product that are very important to the success of your trade show. And you have control over all four.

Know Your Product

I know this sounds like "Business 101," but it's amazing to me and to the buyers I've talked to just how little people know about the product they're selling. In fact, 70 percent of buyers surveyed stated that their biggest complaint about booth personnel was lack of product knowledge.[1]

To illustrate just how important product knowledge is, I'll relate an old story about a large international corporation. Every year it would bring together its top salespeople from around the world for a few days of rest and relaxation as a reward for their contributions. The guest of honor was that year's top producer and he or she would be feted at the last night's banquet. To top the banquet off, this number one salesperson would give the keynote address.

When the time came for the keynote, everyone pulled out pens and paper to write down the pearls of wisdom the "Top

[1] Informal survey of over 200 buyers conducted on my own since 1985.

Gun" would present. Everyone in the audience aspired to be there and didn't want to miss a trick.

As the story goes, one year the number one person, after being introduced, rose slowly and walked to the front amidst a standing ovation. He placed his hands on the podium and looked around the room. His eyes surveyed his surroundings. He remained silent while the people sat down. After the room quieted, he continued to look around. Finally, after several seconds of uncomfortable silence, he began his speech. He said, "I defy anybody in this room to ask me a question about our products that I can't answer." With that, he ended his talk, walked back to his chair, and sat down.

Know your product. It pays.

Demonstrate Your Product

If your product can be demonstrated, then be prepared to do so. Prospects will better understand and appreciate your products if you can show them how they work. Too often at trade shows the booth staff doesn't understand how to operate products. Prospects will most certainly be turned off by this. After all, if you can't show how your own product works, how can they be expected to operate it?

The key to successful demonstration is in three words. Practice, practice, practice. The more you practice demonstrating your product, the better you'll be able to show it off to the show attendees. The more you understand its different capabilities and how they work, the more you'll be able to show each prospect how your product will work for him or her.

The worst time to learn how to demonstrate is the morning of the first day. There is too much going on around you to learn properly, and, frankly, it's too late. Make sure you know how to operate and demonstrate your product before you leave for the show. In addition, if you are in charge of the show, make sure your booth staff members all know, too. Hold a training session at least the day before the show opens to review product demonstrations and floor selling techniques (more on that later in this chapter).

A critical element in demonstration is the product itself. Make sure it works! It's a sure mark of unprofessionalism if you begin a product demonstration and the product doesn't work or perform to expectations. The prospect will be unimpressed or, more likely, uninterested.

Each morning before the show opens, go through a trial demo with your product. Don't just turn it on to see if the lights work; put it through all the paces required for a normal demonstration. Then, if anything goes wrong, you can have it fixed by show time. Things do occasionally go wrong. It's a fact of life that products, no matter how durable, can break down. As an extra precaution, bring at least one backup unit. That way, if something does go wrong, you can quickly direct the prospect to the second model.

Know How Your Product Compares to the Competition's

Trade shows, as I've pointed out earlier, are like shopping malls; attendees can comparison shop among companies. If you make a specific comparison between your product and that of a competitor, it's a simple task for the prospect to walk down the aisle and verify your claim. Because of this opportunity for attendees, it's very important for you to know exactly how you stand with the competition. What new products are they showing? What's their pricing structure? What kind of terms are they offering? How soon are they able to fill orders? What advantages does your product have over theirs? What advantages does their product have over yours? How can you overcome those disadvantages?

As Sun Tzu says in the book *The Art of War* (New York: Delacorte Press, 1983):

> If you know the enemy and yourself, you need not fear the result of a hundred battles. If you know yourself but not the enemy, for every victory gained you will also suffer a defeat. If you know neither the enemy nor yourself, you will succumb in every battle. (18)

That book is 2,500 years old and was written for armies. But its words are just as important in today's battlefield of business.

Show Enthusiasm for Your Product

Even if this sounds corny, it's vital. If you are enthusiastic and excited about your product, it will rub off on your prospects. I've seen salespeople at shows act bored and even apologetic about their products in front of attendees. Why are they at the show? Why do they even work for that company? If you aren't enthusiastic about your own product, then how can you expect anybody else to be?

Staff Meetings and More Training

A Personal Story

Several years ago, I was working as a sales rep for Technicolor's VCR division. I was in my twenties and was the youngest and greenest of the thirty or so salespeople. One January we prepared for the Winter Consumer Electronics Show in Las Vegas.

The day before the show opened, Technicolor held a staff meeting. The purpose of the meeting was to educate us all on the newest products on display at the show and motivate us for successful floor selling. The vice president for sales gave a thorough presentation on the products, carefully explaining all the features and benefits of our entire product line. We sat in a classroom-style setup to listen to his lecture. A few people, including me, took notes. Most didn't.

After hearing about the product line, the president of the corporation walked to the front of the room and introduced a motivational speaker. This man came forward and proceeded to try to motivate us. He talked about how sales was an exciting profession—how we could provide "warm fuzzies" for our customers and how our opportunities for success were unlimited. Needless to say, it didn't work. Despite the fact Technicolor had one of the most innovative product lines in the industry, the show was a disaster. Very few orders were written, and, worse, very few qualified prospects emerged from the thousands who poured into the booth.

Yet, of those few orders, most were written by me. How did this happen? I certainly wasn't some sort of *wunderkind* salesperson. I had not yet shown any special talent for selling. In fact, less than five years earlier, I had been told by another sales manager to get out of sales, because I didn't have the aptitude for it. I wasn't responsible for a large geographic region for Technicolor.

In fact, my territory wasn't geographic at all. It was called "special markets"—mail order and premium/incentive. Both are notorious for the amount of time typically required for closing deals. And I wasn't a particularly aggressive salesperson, either. In fact, at that time in my career, I wasn't even sure I wanted to be a salesperson. I was very intimidated by the whole business.

But, the fact is, I *did* have a successful show—more so than any other salesperson working the Technicolor booth. How did that happen? After all, I attended the same so-called training session with all the other salespeople. What did I learn that nobody else learned? Was I just lucky, or did I have some inside knowledge nobody else had?

In a way, I *did* have some inside knowledge. First, I had already heard the story about the salesperson of the year and his product knowledge. And, whether it was true or not, it made an impression on me. For weeks before the show, I learned everything I could about the Technicolor product line, studying every available piece of material. I talked with Technicolor engineers, asking as many questions as I could. I learned how to operate all the Technicolor products until I could demonstrate them as well as the people who designed them. I learned all about the advantages we had over the competition. In short, I knew our product line cold. I was prepared to answer almost any question a prospect could ask of me.

In addition, I had the benefit of some private tutoring from my father. Having participated in every Consumer Electronics Show since its inception, he taught himself how to work a trade show. He taught me how to dress, how to assume a correct posture, how to project a positive image, how to approach attendees, and how to qualify prospects.

With all that knowledge and training, it was no wonder that I was probably the most enthusiastic salesperson in that booth. I was totally sold on the Technicolor line. I was eager to meet attendees. I helped other salespeople with questions and demonstrations. My enthusiasm was contagious to my customers, and, because of all that, I had a successful show.

I'm not sharing this story with you to show what a great guy I am. The fact is, Technicolor's VCR division went out of business soon after. The purpose of the story is to show you how important *proper* training and education is to the success of your show.

Many companies already have meetings before trade shows and a few even incorporate some training. But *proper* training makes the difference.

Trade shows are expensive. And, as I've stated before, you can't just go to a show, put up your booth, set out your products, hang the corporate logo, and sit back waiting for people to flock to your exhibit. In bad English, it ain't gonna happen.

As I explained earlier, knowing your product line is critical. You need to make sure your booth staff knows that, too; training them on the ins and outs of your products or services is a must before any show. Don't wait until it's too late to educate them. Do it before everyone leaves for the show. Get everybody together for a full day at your facility and give them hands-on training. Let them talk to your engineers or designers or developers. The more information they can learn through actual experiential training and interaction, the more they'll remember.

Some Long-Distance Training Tips

If it's just not feasible to bring the entire staff to your location, then send them as much information as possible. Of course, we all know how difficult it is to make people study independently, so here are a few ideas that may help.

Audio tapes. Put the information on audio tapes. Not just product information, but training for trade shows. This way they can listen to them while driving in their cars. Many people learn better through listening rather than reading, anyway. It's also an effective attention-getter.

Newsletters. Design creative ways of giving them information. Instead of just mailing out reams of paper, how about sending a product newsletter on a monthly basis? It could include information written in a newsy, easy-to-read style, with catchy headlines.

Incentives. Build an incentive for learning. Send out the information along with a quiz. Anybody answering all the questions correctly gets a prize or bonus.

Contests. Create your own "Mystery Prospect" contest for the upcoming trade show. Tell everyone that there will be several planted attendees at the show who will judge each salesperson on his or her presentation. At the end of the show, the one judged to have given the best presentation will win a trip to Hawaii.

Regardless of such efforts, it's still important to have a meeting just prior to the show. The purpose of this meeting should be twofold. First, to explain clearly to everybody what the company's trade show objectives are and what their role is in achieving each one of them. Second, to show them how to accomplish those objectives. The first should have been established before the show. Now you must establish individual responsibilities. Let's look at an example of how this might work.

Your company is planning to exhibit at MACRO-COMM in Chicago. The show will be open four days for a total of twenty-eight hours. Through careful analysis (and help from the formulas in Chapter 1) you plan to rent a twenty-foot by twenty-foot island, a total of 400 square feet. You know the exhibit will take up 120 square feet, leaving you 280 square feet for your people. Knowing that you need approximately fifty square feet per salesperson, you decide on six salespeople ($280 \div 50 = 5.6$ people [round up to 6]). With six people on duty at all times, averaging six qualified contacts per hour each, you achieve thirty-six contacts per hour. By multiplying the number of contacts per hour by total show hours, you get your total show objective:

36 contacts/hr. × 28 hours = 1,008 contacts

Of course, you know that in order to have the most efficient booth staff, you'll need to rotate two shifts of salespeople. That means you'll need twelve salespeople, each working a total of fourteen hours at the show. By dividing the projected number of contacts equally among the twelve salespeople, you'll get their individual objectives:

1,008 contacts divided by 12 = 84 contacts each

You can now tell your salespeople that each one has an objective of eighty-four contacts at the show.

Note: Keep in mind that this is only one way of setting quantifiable show objectives. This particular method only counts show contacts. It doesn't necessarily mean qualified contacts.

By breaking down the corporate objectives in this manner, you establish a way of measuring your progress at the end of each day.

Note: Don't limit yourself to having just one meeting before the show. Have a short meeting each day after the show closes. This way you can find on the spot how everybody did that day in comparison to their goals. In addition, you can share any new information that may be helpful tomorrow, for example, significant new trends, industry announcements, competitor reports, and so forth.

If you really want to stay on top, have a short meeting after every shift comes off the floor. Tally total contacts and give on-the-spot awards to the people who got the most leads.

Factors in Trade Show Success

Once you've clearly stated what is expected of everyone, you can move on to the second part of your preshow meeting—showing them how to accomplish these objectives. Although we'll go into greater detail on boothmanship in Chapter 6, there are a number of other factors to be considered.

A trade show is not a vacation. In a Trade Show Bureau's report, prospects were asked why they attended a trade show.[2] The five reasons given included:

[2] "Trade Show Bureau Research Report No. 13," July 1982.

- To see new products and developments
- General interest in the subject area
- To see a specific product or company
- To attend technical/educational sessions
- To obtain technical or product information

Nowhere in that list do they state vacation as a reason for attending a trade show. Unfortunately, too many salespeople treat shows as just that. While that may have been the case twenty years ago, it certainly isn't now.

During training sessions, people often ask me how long one's hours are at a trade show. My answer is simple. *When you're awake, you're working.* Just because the show hours are 9:00 A.M. to 6:00 P.M. doesn't mean those are the only hours you should be working. Get together with clients and prospects for breakfast before the show opens; it's a great way to start the day. And after the daily meeting, meet customers for drinks and dinner. (It is my opinion that you and your salespeople should refrain from all alcoholic beverages during the show week. Alcohol slows the reflexes and dulls the mind when trying to make intelligent and rational decisions. We've all heard the war stories about trade show parties and revelry. Unfortunately, I've heard about more of those episodes destroying sales opportunities and customer relationships than helping to create such relationships. Maybe twenty to thirty years ago drinking and selling worked together, but not anymore. The buyers and your competition are too sophisticated for that now. Don't take the chance.)

There are plenty of people whom you will want to spend more time with than just the ten minutes at the show. The buyers are there to work the whole show. Take advantage of it! Of course, there's always one other consideration: If your customers and prospects aren't having breakfast or dinner with you, rest assured they're with someone else. Your competition, maybe?

If trade shows aren't vacations, then they shouldn't be incentives. I won a sales contest from my company once. The first prize was an all-expense paid trip to Frankfurt, West Germany, for the annual Frankfurt Messe, a consumer goods show. Our company exhibited at the show each year and the big bosses felt that this was an opportunity to reward the best salespeople.

I flew coach class in a crowded plane from Los Angeles to New York and then to Frankfurt. It took nearly eighteen hours to get there, and I arrived in Frankfurt at 8:00 A.M., local time. After checking in at my hotel, I had to help set up our exhibit, which took all day. I didn't sleep a wink that night because of the time change. The next morning the show opened—for six days, ten hours a day. Some incentive reward.

I guarantee you that the following year I did not win that sales contest. Don't think you're rewarding your salespeople by offering trade shows as incentives. You're not.

Keep the booth clean. One of the biggest turnoffs to prospects is a dirty booth. Make everyone responsible for keeping the booth clean. Keep trash cans and ashtrays emptied, even if it must be done every five minutes. A clean booth is a sign of a company that cares about its appearance; it also denotes professionalism.

Know the objectives. I've already gone over this, but it doesn't hurt to emphasize. It's one thing for the corporate management to know what your objectives are, but it won't do any good if the booth staff doesn't know them. Make sure you clearly define what is expected from your staff. Give everybody clearly defined and quantifiable objectives. Also, have each person come up with some of his or her own personal objectives.

Dress for the best. I call this my *Stan Krangel Rule.* Stan is the executive vice-president for American Express's Direct Merchandising Division. When you get a catalog or merchandise card pack from American Express, there's usually a letter from Stan included. If I wanted to sell a product to Stan at American Express, I wouldn't put on a casual sportcoat and slacks to wear while visiting him in his corner office overlooking the Statue of Liberty in Manhattan. I'd wear my best "sincere" suit and best tie. I want to be taken seriously. For that same reason, if I know Stan is going to be visiting my booth at a trade show, I'm going to dress accordingly. Don't let other so-called experienced trade show salespeople tell you to dress casually for that situation, just because it's a trade show. Make that same good impression on your top prospect.

If there is an exception to this rule, it would be the shoes. You're on your feet all day, for several days. That's hard on the whole body as well as tiring. Wear comfortable shoes with soft soles. There are several shoe manufacturers these days making comfortable dress shoes. Alternatively, put some new Dr. Scholl's footpads in your dress shoes; they'll make a world of difference. Definitely, do not wear new shoes, looking to break them in. You'll be sorry you did!

Don't pass out literature. Have you walked the aisles of a trade show and seen how many people are busy passing out flyers and brochures? Have you ever noticed the loaded bags attendees carry into your booth? Do you really want your literature to get stashed in that pile? The cost of printing today is outrageous, especially if you're using four-color. If you are arbitrarily passing out your literature, you might as well be passing out money.

There are three things that a prospect can do with the flyer you give him or her:

1. Walk around the corner and throw it out. This happens a lot. In fact, you could probably restock your supply of flyers at the end of each day just by retrieving them from the trash cans around the corner.
2. Stuff it in a plastic bag and take it back to the hotel room. Then he or she could spend that night culling through the pile to decide which literature will be taken back on the airplane (you didn't think they'd take it all back did you?). Don't expect a prospect to take too much time reading through all the material he or she has collected, maybe three to five seconds per piece.
3. Put it in a briefcase and take it back to the office, just like you want.

Of these three possibilities, the one with the least chance is the third.

As you meet prospects, tell them you'll send the literature after the show. They'll be happier to hear you say that, because they won't have to worry about it. It makes you look more professional, and it saves you a lot of wasted money. Be sure you then do followup and send the literature immediately after the show. More about that in Chapter 8.

Be ready. Studies have shown that you have about two to three seconds for every ten feet of linear space to attract the prospect's attention. Make sure your people are ready for that moment when the attendee shows interest. This is not a time for shyness, hesitation, or inexperience.

No rookies allowed. The Stan Krangel Rule actually has two parts. Just as the "Dress for the Best" rule, I suggest the following: You certainly wouldn't send a green, inexperienced rookie to call on Stan Krangel in the field. For the same reason, you don't want to have a rookie working your booth at a trade show. When Stan walks in, you want the best salespeople you have to be there waiting for him.

An extension of this rule is sales training. Trade shows are no place for this. The atmosphere is noisy, crowded, intimidating, and highly charged—hardly conducive for training.

If you simply must use trade shows to train your sales staff, then I suggest you do it at small local or regional shows where little harm can be done. You definitely don't want rookies working at your most important show of the year. Also, if you're waiting until the show is open to train people for floor selling, it's too late.

CHAPTER 6

Working with Your Staff

Boothmanship

I finished up the last chapter by stressing that a trade show is no place for sales training. Your corporate investment in the show is high. This is simply not the place to risk that investment. You want your booth staff to be ready for action, to take advantage of every opportunity to reach your objective.

Although there are many similarities between field sales and trade show sales, there are also many contrasts. Let's look, again, at some of those differences.

In the field, you go to the buyer. At a trade show, they come to you. Just think about it. Buyers from all over the world (or at least from all over your region) might be coming to the show to find answers to their problems, look for new products, and learn about their industry. What an incredible opportunity! Rather than traveling to see them, they are traveling to see you. That's a great advantage.

In the field, you are on their turf. At a trade show, they are on yours. This observation, of course, has much to do with the power game we all play. When you are meeting a client or prospect at his/her office, the client is in control. There can be quite a few distractions. It's not unusual for the client to get phone calls, unexpected visitors, or have a secretary come in and out with messages, coffee, or the mail. Although trade shows definitely have distractions, the buyer is out of his/her comfort zone. The distractions don't belong to his/her company; in fact, you can design your booth so that the only distractions the buyer sees are purposely put there by you. You control the environment; you can create any atmosphere you want. You hold the power.

The field is not always conducive to demonstrations. A trade show is perfect for demonstrations. Selling earthmovers, for example. Well, they are a little bit difficult to get into a prospect's office. You can show them lots of shiny eight-by-ten colored glossies backed up with a few dozen testimonials, but there's nothing like a trade show for demonstrations. You can let them climb all over that earthmover. You can set up a real life demonstration at a show; bring in a few tons of dirt and let the prospect move it around himself.

Furthermore, you can develop a multimedia presentation along with the product that will impress your prospects. That's tough to do in somebody's small private office.

At a trade show, you can see more prospects in one hour than you'll see all week in the field. Trade shows do not require driving around looking for nonexistent addresses. There is no waiting in an impersonal lobby with a dozen other salespeople. Buyers come to you at a trade show, and they come to you en masse. As soon as you're done talking to one prospect, along comes another one! Depending on your product and marketplace, you can see six, ten, even fifteen prospects every hour. That's a gold mine.

At a trade show, prospects are more relaxed and in the buying mode. They're away from the distractions of the office; it's probably a nice break for them. We all have several responsibilities at the office and buyers are no exception. They simply don't spend 100 percent of their time buying. They are there for very specific reasons—to solve problems, see new technology, visit possible vendors. Their minds are on the show and not back at the office.

At a trade show, you are forced to make a lot of cold calls. Many of us just don't like to make cold calls, and for that reason a lot of time in the field is spent with people we know. Very little time is spent in face-to-face contact with total strangers. At a trade show, contact with lots of strangers is standard. For many of us that's a very uncomfortable situation—but it's necessary if business is to expand.

You have less time to meet with prospects at a trade show. It's not unusual to spend a lot of time with prospects in the field. Sometimes we'll be with them for several hours. Unfortunately, we don't have the luxury of time at a trade show. There are only a finite number of minutes at a show and we need to see as many people as possible in that time. Quite often we'll spend as little as ten minutes with a prospect and many times much less.

The cost of closing a sale in the field is more than four times as expensive as at a trade show. Every time an industrial salesperson calls on a client, it costs his employer $229.70, according to a study on 1985 costs conducted by the McGraw-Hill Laboratory of Advertising Performance. That same study reported that the average number of sales calls required to close an order was 5.5, a total of $1,263.35.[1] Compare those figures to the "Trade Show Bureau's Research Reports No. 18" and "No. 2020." Every time a salesperson makes contact with a qualified prospect at a trade show, it costs $106.89. In addition, the average number of follow-up calls needed to close a sale is 0.8, with 54 percent of all leads closed without a personal sales call.[2] Even with the follow-up call, the total cost of that sale is only $290.65—less than one-fourth the cost in the field!

Of course, there are many other differences, but these certainly give you a good idea about the contrasts. And because of these, both you and your salespeople need to learn how to properly work a trade show exhibit.

Exhibit Selling Steps

What happens during the five-to-ten-minute interaction between an attendee and a salesperson? How can a salesperson

---

[1]McGraw-Hill Lab of Advertising Performance (1985). Specific source is the "Trade Show Bureau Research Report No. 2020," July 1986.

[2]"Trade Show Bureau Research Report No. 18," April 1983, and "No. 2020," July 1986.

properly prepare for this short encounter so as to get the most out of it? The first step is to break the process down and get an overview of what is happening.

As with any meeting in social or business situations, there first needs to be some type of opening. In a trade show, this would simple be some nonthreatening conversation with the attendee. Once the conversation has begun, it's important to move quickly into the qualification/presentation step: Who are you talking to? What are his needs? How can you help him? Once you have covered these steps and the prospect acknowledges the possibility of working with you, then move into the final step: the close. The close is simply asking for action toward your show objective. For example, if your objective is to gather leads for later follow-up, then your close would be to get the prospect to commit to a personal call after the show.

Let's analyze each step in the process.

The Opening

Have you ever walked into a booth at a trade show and practically been accosted by one of the booth staff? He or she homes in on you like a heat-seeking missile and immediately launches into a sales pitch without any regard for you as a person. It reminds me of the stereotypical used-car salesman. We're all turned off by such behavior.

Do you remember playing tag as a kid? When my friends and I played, we always had a safe zone called *home*. As long as we were touching that safe zone, the person who was "it" couldn't get us. Attendees at trade shows have their own safe zone, too. It's the aisle. And as long as they are walking in the aisle, they feel safe from the attacks of booth personnel, free to examine the exhibits without fear of being disturbed.

As I wrote earlier, trade shows are very uncomfortable for all of us. We are usually in a strange, noisy location, surrounded by people we don't know. It can be a little bit frightening! As booth personnel, we must do whatever we can to make an attendee feel comfortable with us. We must appear nonthreatening.

Attendees often walk with what I call the *trade show pace and gaze*. They stroll through the aisles with their eyes fixed on one of two levels. They're either looking for products displayed at waist-high levels, or signs about eight feet high. In other words, they aren't looking at you! In fact, they will do everything they can to avoid looking a salesperson in the eye. Therefore, an initial objective is to break the attendee out of his/her hypnotic step and stare. For the most part, the booth design and product presentation (if done effectively) will take care of breaking the pace. The exhibit's responsibility is to slow the attendee down; the salesperson then takes over and captures his/her attention.

The attendee is a person and wants to be treated as such. The first step in the trade show selling process is to put the attendee at ease. Therefore, the opening line should not be a selling line. It needs to be a comfortable icebreaker that shows the attendee you understand he/she is a human being.

By looking at the name badge, you may find an easy opener. Some examples of opening lines are:

- "Hi, I see you're from Tucson. I went to school there. Is the Tack Room still open?"
- "How are you enjoying the show so far?"
- "Hi, I see you work for Consolidated Marketing. Do you know Marv and Sherwin?"
- "Whew, are your feet as tired as mine?"
- "I can't believe how big this show is! Have you been through much of it yet?"

Openers slow attendees down and get them talking. You want to be as natural as possible; don't sound mechanical. In other words, don't use the same opener with every person you meet or, after a while, you'll sound like a broken record.

Four qualifications for Effective Opening Lines:

1. It must break preoccupation. An attendee has many other things on her mind. She may be thinking the show is overwhelming, or that she shouldn't be away from the office. Remembering appointments and thinking about possible purchases are also distracting thoughts. Your opener needs to break that preoccupation and get attention focused on you.
2. It must focus on the individual. Again, the idea here is to make the attendee feel important. By making a positive

comment about him or asking his opinion, you make him feel good.

3. It must create a bond between you and the attendee. The attendee is being bombarded with thousands of "buy me" signals throughout the show. By initiating conversation with a nonthreatening gesture, the attendee will feel more comfortable with you, thus creating a mutual bond.

4. It must let both of you play a little. We're all on our guard at trade shows, especially the attendees, who are being perpetually accosted. An effective opener brings a brief respite to the sensory overload they're experiencing. Introduce a short joke about the show, the exhibits, the other attendees, or life, in general.

While brainstorming openers during one of my recent seminars at a high-tech company, one participant shared this opener, "Can I help confuse you some more today?" It certainly fits all four criteria.

Sometimes, No Opener Is Necessary

Once in a great while a hot prospect appears who looks like a hot prospect from the very start. He walks into your exhibit as if he works there. He goes directly to the product that interests him and looks at it. He may even pick it up to examine it closely. He exudes the air of "I'm a real buyer. Will someone please take my order." And, of course, the booth personnel climb over each other to get to this prospect.

Someone showing that much interest does not need an opening line. The best approach is to respond with interest in the visitor and his needs by moving right to the qualifying step. Use an open-ended question, such as, "I see you're interested in our new four-pronged widget. Do you have a need for it in your work?" Obviously, it's easy to engage this type of attendee. Just remember, he or she is rare. Too many salespeople stand around an exhibit waiting for this type of visitor to arrive. Don't be like that!

Two caveats about the eager-beaver prospect: First, be sure to get control of the conversation as soon as possible. If you let the prospect dominate you, you may never get to the qualifying step. Briefly answer any questions the prospect asks, but immediately follow up with a qualifying question. Second, beware the competition! They may come spying for information and act like interested prospects. Make sure you move into the qualifying step quickly, before you give away any proprietary information.

The Qualifying/Presentation Step

After getting their attention, move quickly into the qualifying step of the selling process. Remember that time is a precious commodity, especially at a trade show. Don't think in terms of how many hours the show is open; think in terms of minutes. If a trade show is open a total of twenty-six hours, for example, look at it as 1,560 minutes. If you work at 100 percent efficiency and top speed, you'll see a new attendee every six minutes, or 260 people total for the show. But none of us are 100 percent efficient; none of us can go top speed all the time. Some hours are slower than others. You might only be 75 percent efficient. Some attendees will take more than six minutes of your time. There are many factors influencing how many people you talk to. But be as efficient and effective as possible, and when you control the situation, you can be just that. That's why it's so important not to waste time and to move into the qualifying step as soon as possible.

As I pointed out in "The Opening," a good place to look for help is the name badge. Use it as you did in the opener. If you know something about the company, it could be helpful in qualifying the attendee. Ask what area the attendee works in. What are his or her responsibilities? Once you find that out, you can determine how your product may help that company, and whether he or she has the authority to influence the buying decision. If you don't know anything about the company, then find out more.

Some shows color code badges. At the 1988 Winter Consumer Electronics Show, badges were color coded as follows:

- Red for the Exhibitors
- Orange for the Manufacturers
- Purple for the Manufacturer's Reps
- Turquoise for the Retailers
- Brown for the Distributors
- Navy Blue for the Department/Chain Store Buyers
- Mauve for the Institutional Buyers

- Aqua for the Premium/Catalog Buyers
- Yellow for the Editorial Press
- Tan for the Media Representatives
- Green for the Advertising, Marketing, and PR/Consultants
- Gray for the Financial/Market Analysts
- Lavender for the Guests

What a great way to help prequalify attendees! Of course, it doesn't help if you're color-blind.

If you exhibit at a show with color-coded badges, be sure to include that information in your preshow meetings with your staff. Specifically target certain badge colors and let the others alone. For example, you might only be interested in talking to retailers, catalogers, and department store buyers. By instructing your staff to be on the lookout for turquoise, navy blue, and aqua badges, you effectively screen out many people walking by. After all, you don't want to waste your time with unqualified prospects. If the show doesn't have color-coded badges, and most of them don't, then it's up to you to carry the responsibility for qualifying the attendee.

Why qualify leads? There are three reasons for qualifying at a trade show. The first is economics. Every contact you make with a prospect costs money. By qualifying at a show, you save money. The second is time. Just as every sales contact costs money, it also costs time. We all know that timing often has much do to with the success of making a sale. By delaying the qualifying process until after a show, the chance arises that a competitor might close a deal with a prospect first. By qualifying at a show, you keep one step ahead of the competition. The third reason is ease. My father used to tell me to follow the K.I.S.S. principle— Keep It Simple, Salesman. He told me that if it's possible to eliminate any unnecessary steps in the process, it saves headaches and potential problems. Change K.I.S.S. to Q.I.S.S.— Qualifying Is Smart Selling.

What if you can't qualify at a show? Once in a great while a company can't qualify at a show. Usually, one of two factors cause this situation. The first is that the product is a runaway hit and appeals to nearly everybody at the show. The second reason is that the company has a small sales force. Of course, a combination of both factors is a good problem to have.

MicroDisk Services of Redmond, Washington, had such a situation in New York at the June 1988 PC Expo. With only two salespeople staffing the booth, it had a product that many attendees were interested in. The crowds were so large that it wasn't unusual for a salesperson to give a presentation to fifty people at once. An impossible situation for qualifying each contact! The solution came from Molin/Cutler Telemarketing Services of Seattle. MicroDisk turned over nearly 1,000 leads from the show and let Molin/Cutler's trained telemarketing reps qualify for them. By determining the strongest prospects, MicroDisk was then able to give those leads to their in-house people for solid follow-up. Within one month of the show these efforts generated more than $1 million in signed business with fifteen national accounts, plus another $1 million expected within the next twelve months.

What does qualified mean? The definition of qualified depends on your own objectives. If, for example, your main show objective is to generate new leads and the only prospect you're looking for is a department store buyer, then a navy blue badge may be all you need to qualify him. Then again, you may have a more horizontal market and are looking for anyone who uses PCs in the office. In that case, you are merely looking for purchase probability. You may have a product with a short shelf life. In that case, you are looking for purchase probability within a specific time frame. Such diversity makes it imperative that you define what qualified means to you; then make sure your entire staff understands it.

A Golf Analogy

Many years ago, before I joined the real world, I used to be a PGA golf professional. One of the most valuable lessons I learned as a player was to plan each hole backward before I played it.

Imagine, for example, you are golfing on a par four hole. (*Par* basically refers to the length of a hole. A par four is long enough for it to require a minimum of two shots to reach the green and an average of two putts to get the ball into the hole.) An average golfer will play the hole in the fashion referred to as *tee-to-green*. In other words, he will plan to hit his first shot (the *drive*) as far as possible. After he has done that, he then plans how to play his next shot to the green. The length and direction of the first shot determines what type of club he uses in his second shot. He then hits the second shot toward the hole and, as before, his third shot depends on the length and direction of his second. When he finally reaches the green he then plans his putts.

As a professional tournament player, however, I first play the hole backward in my mind. Using the same par four as an example, I determine where the hole is on the green and where I want to putt from. Greens are often rolling and slanted and there are certain spots from which it is easier to putt. After determining where I want my ball to be on the green, I go backward down the fairway and find the ideal location for my ball to be in order to hit it to that selected spot on the green. Again, there will be a location best suited for this task. Once I've selected this location I now know where I want to aim my first shot from the tee. It's not unusual for this method to completely change the type of club used at the tee and in the fairway.

Just like the golf professional who plays "green-to-tee," a trade show sales professional works backward in determining how to qualify a prospect. Ask yourself who the ideal customer is. What is that person like? What characteristics does that person possess? What position does she hold in the company? What size company does she work for? How many people report to her? What size data base does she work with? How many stores does she own? Does she have a need to send documents overnight? How often does she use her telephone? Where is she located? How big is her budget?

Get out a pencil and write down a detailed description of your ideal customer. You can use a separate piece of paper, but if you fill in the blanks that follow, you'll always know where to look.

You may want to create such a description for every show you exhibit at. Because many shows are geared to a specific vertical market, your targets may vary from show to show.

My ideal customer:

1. _____

_____

2. _____

_____

3. _____

_____

4. _____

_____

5. _____

_____

6. _____

_____

Leading Questions

Once you've described your ideal customer in detail, work backward to ask leading questions that will give you the information necessary to qualify potential customers. Be sure these are open-ended questions, beginning with Who? What? Where? When? Why? How? How much? How many? and Which? Following are some specific questions that may help you develop your criteria for prospects.

■ Who is involved in the decision-making process?

- What are his specific responsibilities?
- Where is her company located? Is it within our geographical distribution area?
- When does he anticipate a need for this type of product?
- Why is she interested in our product?
- How do they plan to utilize this new product?
- How much money do they have in their budget?
- How many people will be using this product?
- Which area of the company will use it the most?

While you are qualifying an attendee, take the opportunity to present your product in light of how it will help in several of these areas. Gear your responses to specific needs, focusing on specific problem areas the prospect may have. That's true selling.

When asking these types of open-ended questions, you control the conversation. This is important. There are only two directions to go after the qualifying step. One is to determine that this visitor is not a qualified lead, at which point you politely end the conversation and move on to the next attendee. The second direction is to determine that this visitor is a qualified prospect. If this is the case and you present your product as a problem solver during the conversation, the prospect should see its value.

Remember the lead card example back in Chapter 3? This is the time to pull it out and put the information in writing. Do it as soon as you determine you are talking with a qualified prospect. Waiting until after the conversation ends to write information down is a mistake. There are four very good reasons to fill out a lead card while interviewing a prospect:

1. Memory is unreliable. How much can you forget within a few minutes? Plenty. Plus, with the circuslike distractions of a trade show, it's doubly hard to remember specific points of discussion. Write them down while you're talking with the prospect.
2. Time is valuable. Remember, you only have a finite number of minutes at a trade show. Even if it only takes a couple of minutes to scribble a few notes after a prospect leaves, you are wasting time. If you average 9.5 minutes on each prospect contact, that comes to 6.3 contacts per hour, or 176 contacts for a twenty-eight-hour show; if you add two more minutes to each contact to fill out the lead card, the time

spent per contact comes to 11.5 minutes; that's only 5.2 contacts per hour, or 146 total show contacts. That's a 17 percent loss of contacts. It's not worth it. Write the information down while talking to a prospect.

3. It's professional. Prospects are impressed, not insulted when a salesperson takes notes. They feel it demonstrates a real interest in getting the right facts. And, as a matter of fact, you are.

4. It creates a sense of obligation in the prospect. Your goal in this conversation may be to set a follow-up appointment for after the show. Once you've begun to write down information on a lead card, you've created a sense of obligation with the prospect to at least be willing to go to that next step.

During the Qualifying/Selling step remember that you are not giving a complete sales presentation; you are only presenting an overview of how your particular product can help a prospect based on one or two specific needs. You're not trying to make the sale, you're trying to accomplish your objective. This is one of the big differences between field selling and trade show selling. In the field, you may be used to more relaxed interactions, controlled in large part by the prospect. At the trade show, you must control the situation and keep it short.

Exceptions to these rules arise, and you should keep your eye out for them. The prospect who is truly in a buying mode and could possibly be sold at the show deserves more time and attention. The big buying team that is comparison shopping at the show and potentially represents a sizable order is another example. Be alert for these opportunities and exceptions.

If you do run into one of these situations, use time away from the show to close the deal. Meet at your hotel or over dinner to iron out the details. This practice gives both of you the opportunity to utilize the show fully, and it provides you with an unhurried, distraction-free atmosphere.

The Close

After a nonthreatening opening, and a thorough job of presenting your product and qualifying the prospect, the close naturally follows. If your objective is to get the prospect to agree to a follow-up sales call after the show, all you need to do is ask for an appointment.

Basically, all you're doing in the close is restating the prospect's needs and reiterating how your products will help satisfy
those needs. Then you follow with a statement like, "Then you
would agree that we should meet again in two weeks to discuss
this further?" Even though it's short and simple, this step is important. By closing you establish future contact with the prospect. If you go through steps one and two without the close, you
risk losing a potential sale. In a sense, the trade show close is
much like closing in the field, with one notable difference; at the
show, you close on an appointment, not the product.

Team Signals

Every once in a while, you will run into a circumstance outside
of show selling that still requires teamwork. There are two common situations:

The "**Leech.**" This is actually a not-so-nice term for an unqualified attendee who won't let you go. Politely tell him you've
enjoyed the conversation, but you know he wants to see other
exhibits and you need to get back to work. It usually works. In a
situation where the person doesn't take the hint, use a team signal. A prearranged signal—a tug on the ear, a finger across the
nose (a la *The Sting*), whatever—can indicate your predicament
to a booth mate. Once a co-worker picks it up, she can approach
you with a reminder of a fictitious appointment or some other de-
vious device. The point is to get you away as quickly as possible.

The "**Complainer.**" Occasionally, somebody has a problem
with your accounts receivable department and decides to take it
up personally with the president of your company. Often the intention is to simply make a scene at a crowded show with the no-
tion that it will hurt your business. Without going into a
complete discussion of what planet we should blast these nasties
off to, it's important to plan for them. If such a situation arises,
the first thing to do is get the person out of your exhibit as
quickly as possible. One way of doing this is to appoint a daily
ombudsman responsible for handling the unhappy person. Have
the appointed troubleshooter take the person out for a cup of
coffee over which to listen to his problems.

Nonverbal Communication

A trade show may be as small as a few dozen exhibits or as large as several thousand. In either case, attendees walking through the aisles are no more comfortable being surrounded by strangers than you are. Because of this, it's important to be aware of the fine art of nonverbal communication.

Attendees walking through the exhibit area move at the *trade show pace*. At the same time, they develop the *trade show gaze*, mentally culling out exhibits, effectively eliminating different booths from consideration. They may do this without even stopping to talk with us. Or they may do it within fifteen seconds of meeting us! In effect, they are looking for reasons to cross us off their list.

I learned something interesting from my good friend George Walther, one of the country's leading telemarketing experts. In his seminars, George will often pair people up with a total stranger, turn out the lights, and have the two people talk to each other. George will have the two discuss a very ordinary topic— what their favorite dessert is, the last vacation they had, their respective hobbies. George only lets the first person talk for about thirteen seconds, then switches for another thirteen seconds.

After this little exercise, George then shows the audience a list of adjectives. Included in the list are such words as shy, confident, assertive, sharing, thoughtful, caring, honest, intelligent, and friendly. The two people then select three or four words from the list that would describe their partner. People are amazed at how accurately others can read them in less than a quarter of a minute, after only hearing their voices!

Obviously George is showing people how our telephone voice sounds, but the same type of "instant analyzation" is going on when we meet people at a trade show. And because of the very nature of trade shows, a brief encounter is usually all we get with an attendee. Research has shown that 80 percent of the way an attendee remembers your exhibit is based on the behavior of the booth staff.[3] Because that encounter is so brief, nonverbal com-

[3] A number of exhibit managers, and show management companies, have conducted research on attendee purchase behavior and the effect of booth personnel on show performance.

municative skills are probably more important at trade shows than in any other selling situation.

Body Language—The Prospect

Before we consider how to improve our body language, let's learn to read the body language of attendees. As visitors walk by your booth, watch for those subliminal signals that will open the door for the first approach. Watch how they walk, stand, and use their hands. Look at their eyes. Do they look like they want to talk? Remember the trade show pace and gaze? Attendees get into this steady pace at a show to protect themselves. But once something has caught their eyes, it breaks the pace. Keep your own eye open for this break. If it's in front of your booth, it's probably something you're displaying that slows them down. Once you see that, it's time to engage.

Notice how they stand. Do their shoulders still aim down the aisle or have they squared them into your display? The more their body shows an inclination toward your exhibit, the more interested they are.

Watch for hand and arm signals from the prospect:

Palm rubbing. This is a positive sign, usually of eagerness, anticipation, or anxiousness. Follow the signal and move ahead.

Touching the face. This action means a person is thinking about what you've just said, maybe about how your product will fit into an office system. The best action here is to be quiet and wait for the prospect to take the next lead.

Steepling. Have you ever been with a person who puts his elbows on a chair's armrest and steeples his hands? This is one of the most powerful subliminal gestures a person can make. It represents power, knowledge, and confidence. A prospect who uses this signal knows what he wants, and, apparently, you're giving the right information. If he is steepling and touching his face, it's a very good sign of interest. Be careful not to use this signal yourself too early in the conversation. You might come across as cocky.

Arms folded. This action is a classic protective gesture. People who use this are saying, "Don't bother me." Perhaps you haven't made your visitor feel comfortable. Slow down your presentation and work on assuring your customer before you proceed any further. Be more casual and empathetic toward the attendee. Once the arms are relaxed, move on with the process.

Clenched fists. I don't have to tell you this is a bad signal. Use the same tactics to regain your client's interest that you would with crossed arms.

Legs crossed at ankles. This may be a defensive gesture by the prospect, much like crossed arms. Handle it the same way. Be careful, though; the prospect may just be tired from a long day. According to the Trade Show Bureau, a visitor spends more than eight hours on the show floor a day.[4] That's a lot of time on the feet. So, if ankles are crossed, watch to see if the prospect also shifts weight from foot to foot; if so, it's indicative of weariness, in which case you've got to work a little harder to hold the prospect's attention.

Sudden changes in gestures. Don't automatically assume that any of the above gestures are good or bad. Are his arms crossed? Maybe he's cold, not defensive. Maybe you're cold, too.

The thing to watch for is an abrupt change in body language. If he seemed open and comfortable with you and then suddenly folded his arms, it might have been something you just said or showed. Stop the presentation and say something like, "I see you're concerned. Did I say something that bothers you?" or, "You seem bothered about our terms. Would you share your concerns with me?"

Become a student of prospects and be aware of any changes in their subliminal signals. If you miss one of these signals and continue your presentation, you could lose a prospect.

---

[4]"Trade Show Bureau Research Report No. 21," May 1984.

Proxemics

Proxemics is the study of personal space. The important thing to understand in regard to proxemics is the comfort zone and how it relates to the selling process. There are three distinct zones extending outward from each one of us. (See Figure 6–1.)

The outermost zone, known as the *public zone*, begins approximately twelve feet away from us and extends outward. Anybody in this zone is not deemed to be someone to pay attention to. In other words, it's not important for us to acknowledge anyone who is twelve feet or farther away. In a trade show, you wouldn't be able to sell somebody your product if he were farther than twelve feet away. Conversely, an attendee knows that he is safe as long as he keeps his distance.

The middle zone, known as the *personal zone*, extends from approximately three to twelve feet away. Anybody entering this zone can now be attended to. At a trade show, this zone is where the selling process begins. When an attendee allows you to enter this zone, you are given unspoken permission to begin communicating. Opening and qualifying steps take place in this zone.

Figure 6–1 Our Personal Space

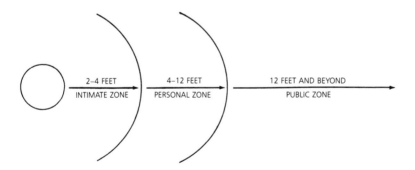

2–4 FEET
INTIMATE ZONE

4–12 FEET
PERSONAL ZONE

12 FEET AND BEYOND
PUBLIC ZONE

The closest zone, known as the *intimate zone,* extends up to three or four feet away from the body. This is where selling occurs. If someone allows you to enter this zone while you're talking about your product, you will have a much easier time of selling.

Have you ever heard the phrase, "an arm's length transaction"? An arm's length is approximately three feet, so the phrase could be translated into, "Don't let him get near your intimate zone!" Be sure and respect the attendee's personal space. Don't move in too close too quickly. Wait until you receive signals giving you permission. If the prospect touches you on the arm while in conversation, it's a positive sign. Likewise, if he leans toward you while listening to your presentation, he's giving you permission to lean in, too.

One last word about proxemics. Just as animals in the jungle stake out territory, so will humans. Be very careful you don't do that in your exhibit. Don't leave any of your personal things—briefcase, notepad, date book—around for people to see. They send a territorial signal. Keep such things out of sight. The exhibit is meant to be warm and inviting to the attendee, not threatening.

Body Language—The Booth Staff

Have you ever heard the phrase, "You never get a second chance to make a good first impression"? Trade shows exemplify the truth in such phrases. The communication process begins before attendees even step into our exhibit. By consciously sending warm, confident, positive signals at all times, we tell attendees that we are someone worth knowing. Let's look at how nonverbals affect our performance and how we can use them to our advantage.

The Stance

When standing in the booth waiting for a prospect (yes, I said *standing*—never sit!), your stance alone tells the prospect a lot. Stand with your feet about shoulder width apart, weight evenly balanced, and your hands either hanging at your side or clasped behind your back. Such a stance is open and powerful.

Don't shift your weight from foot to foot or cross your legs at the ankles. These are very weak positions, indicative of defensiveness to an attendee. It's hard to keep from doing this when your feet are tired at the end of a long show day, but that visitor at 4:00 P.M. may be your biggest catch of the day. Remain alert! One way to control this distracting practice is to wear comfortable shoes during the show. A show is not the place to break in a new pair! (Reread the section in Chapter 5, "Dress for the Best.")

If you have anything to say about booth design and construction, buy a good pad to go under your carpet. Not only will you feel a big difference in your own legs and feet, but so will the attendees. They'll spend more time in your exhibit and they won't know why. Another subliminal selling technique.

The Handshake

Ah, the almighty handshake. I have actually had buyers tell me they didn't order from a particular salesperson because of his/ her handshake. Its importance cannot be overstated.

The handshake is how you and the prospect measure each other's strength and purpose. If you have a weak, sweaty, fragile, trembling grip, the prospect immediately assumes you are a pushover; he'll feel confident that he can turn you down and send you on your way. If your grip is weak, build it up. Get one of those hand/forearm exercisers at a sporting goods store, or just squeeze an old tennis ball to death. To combat sweaty palms, wash your hands frequently, don't clasp them together while standing around, and leave them out of your pockets; let the air dry them out. Carry moist towelettes so you won't have to constantly leave the booth to wash your hands. Also, don't let an attendee see you wiping them on your clothes—an instant loss of points.

Offer your hand first to your visitor, but wait for him or her to let go first. Never end a handshake too early. Don't use the two-handed shake unless you know the person well. People tend to be suspicious of someone using that type of "politician's" handshake at the first meeting. Shake hands firmly, but not bone-crushingly. Some people want to show off how strong they are. It's unnecessary and annoying.

Men. When you first meet an attendee, a useful trick to use in gaining control quickly is to pull the prospect toward you a little as you shake. It shows warmth and lack of fear. Don't worry if he or she pulls back slightly. You've established who's in control of the upcoming conversation. I do not recommend women try this. Unfortunately, if a man is on the receiving end, he may interpret it as an advance. A woman receiving such a handshake from another woman may be put off.

Women. If your hand is small and you're shaking hands with a large person, spread your fingers a slight bit, giving the impression of a larger grip. This helps to keep your receiver from seeing you as small and frail.

Hands and Arms

While waiting for an attendee, stand with your hands at your side or clasped behind your back. Never cross your arms or put your hands in your pockets. These positions send out a very defensive or an "I don't care" signal. While engaging a prospect, use open-palmed gestures with your elbows away from your body. This denotes a warm, welcoming posture.

When listening, keep your hands unclenched and visible. This sends a nonverbal message of, "I trust you and you can trust me." Don't take the chance of scaring off a visitor. The first minute is crucial to the success of the encounter. Once you've made an attendee feel comfortable and confident through your opening and qualifying steps, you'll be in a better position to move quickly into the close.

Eye Contact

The salesperson at a trade show must make a special effort to maintain solid eye contact with the person to whom he is talking. There are so many other interesting things to look at and so many faces going by that the temptation to look everywhere except in your prospect's eyes is very strong. Many of us have been told to maintain pseudo eye contact by looking at a point on the tip of a person's nose or at the middle of his forehead. This process of depersonification is frequently counterproductive. People know when someone is looking into their eyes, and will sense when you are not.

When you look in someone's eyes, you tend to check one eye, then the other. When you stare at a nose, your eyes are locked onto one point; the prospect will sense something is wrong. If you are standing face to face and closer than five feet apart at a show, a prospect with normal vision will be able to see that you aren't looking into his eyes. So, avoid tricks that can only hurt your chances by offending a potential lead. Look directly into your prospect's eyes and maintain that connection.

Subliminal Selling

People like to communicate with people who are like them. Talk to them in their style and show you care for them as individuals. Reaching this harmonious connection in a brief few minutes can be done; it brings trust, which in turn gains sales. If you use rapport skills, opportunities will come to you.

Rapport is the bridge that helps the person you're communicating with find meaning and intent in the things you say. It helps them feel comfortable with you and creates a feeling of warmth and understanding. Most importantly, when it comes to selling, rapport helps your prospects feel that what you're saying is directed right at them, aimed at their particular needs and desires. Without rapport, you're just communicating information. You might as well just read your presentation to the customer. The best way to generate rapport is to care genuinely and sincerely about what your prospect needs or desires. No technique will work unless you really care about the person you're dealing with.

I can't show you how to care, but I can explain some verbal and nonverbal techniques that develop rapport quickly:

Mirroring. People tend to do business with or put their most trust in people who are like them. If you are radically different from the attendee, it will take longer to build the warmth and trust necessary to make a sale. One of the ways you can quickly build trust and rapport is to mirror body movement and posture.

If you observe people who enjoy being around each other, you'll notice an unconsciously high amount of physical rapport.

Adversaries, on the other hand, will often deliberately, though unconsciously, mismatch movements. They'll even go so far as to break eye contact to prevent rapport from accidentally being created.

During any interaction with an attendee, watch his body movements closely. If he crosses his arms, cross yours. If he puts his arms by his side, put your arms by your side. When he leans forward, lean forward, too. If you do this very subtly, your prospect will have no idea of what you are doing, and you'll be amazed at how quickly high rapport between you occurs. Mirroring body movements is really a by-product of having incredibly high rapport.

Matching. Matching involves using key words and phrases that hold significance for your customer. People have a style of talking and a particular set of words that are meaningful to them. If you can identify their style and key phrases, you'll have the key to unlock their mind.

Different industries have their own style of talking. Attorneys have "legalese" and stock brokers have "brokerese." The particular industry your prospect belongs to will have a vocabulary peculiar to itself. Be sure to learn his key words and phrases so you'll be able to communicate more effectively. A good example of jargon is the word *networking*. This is a very overused term in entrepreneurial circles these days, but a different version of the term is used in other industries. In the real estate market, the word *farming* means the same thing. And in some questionable industries, the nasty word *pyramiding* has been used interchangeably with networking.

Verbal rapport. The best way to establish verbal rapport with an attendee is to listen intently for the first minute or so, making a mental note of what you hear. Listen for inflection patterns, length of sentences, and certain key words or phrases. This information will help you understand them subliminally by allowing you to duplicate speaking patterns. Don't be too concerned about duplicating an attendee's style of speaking. As long as you're not mimicking them in a sarcastic manner, they'll hardly notice. People expect you to talk the way they do. When you don't communicate in a style that is comfortable to the prospects, you're the one who is causing tension, not them.

Anchoring. This is more or less a reverse style of matching for building rapport. When anchoring a prospect, you are using a key word, phrase, or physical movement of your own to anchor specific good feelings and emotions. For example, when I speak before a group, I'll often begin by telling a humorous story about my past experience as a professional golfer. Usually the story is about something that, at the time, was embarrassing, but is now funny. As I hit the punch line I'll make a certain face, usually a look of naive bewilderment to match the look on my face at the time of the incident. Usually, the combination of how I tell the story and the face I make will draw laughter from the audience.

The interesting thing that then happens is that during my subsequent speech or seminar, I can make that same face to draw laughter. I've learned to use that face to elicit good feelings at specific times during the course of the program. What's happening is that the people in the audience, through my initial story, have been subconsciously programmed to believe that when I make that face, they are supposed to feel good. I've anchored that face with the good feeling.

The same effect can be achieved with a certain word or phrase. Comedian Joan Rivers uses, "Can we talk?" Ronald Reagan uses, "There you go again." Rodney Dangerfield says, "I get no respect."

In a selling situation, if it's possible to anchor a word or physical movement to a good feeling with the prospect, it's possible to elicit that same feeling when you're trying to close the sale.

A salesperson used this technique on me at a local Nordstrom department store. I was looking for a new suit recently, when I decided to stop in and try some on. The salesperson who walked up to help came straight out and said, "You're very handsome!" While I was basking in the compliment and thanking her, she touched me lightly on the elbow. First, she took the chance of invading my intimate zone; I didn't mind, however, because of the compliment. Second, she anchored my good feelings by touching my elbow.

I wasn't having any success with the $200 to $300 suits, when she suggested I try on a $600 suit. I reluctantly agreed to do it, knowing full well I was wasting her time and mine. I'd never spend that kind of money on a suit! As I came out of the dressing area, she walked right up and commented, "That suit looks great on you!" And, you guessed it, she touched me on the elbow exactly like she had earlier. The suit did look great on me, but her touching my elbow helped elicit the same good feelings I felt when she said I was handsome. I bought the suit.

A Word about Nonverbal Communication

The little tricks taught in this chapter are not for everybody. If you feel uncomfortable about using them, then don't. Your first and foremost objective is to help the customer, not con him. These subliminal techniques are very powerful in helping you develop an early rapport with a prospect, but if you don't have a strong desire to help your customer solve problems, then these tools will only be misused.

CHAPTER 7

Secrets of Successful Shows

Quickie Trade Show Tips

Don't Sit

If you sit during a trade show, you give attendees the impression that you don't care, that you don't want to be bothered. Attendees will not interrupt your private time, as they perceive it. Remember, attendees are also looking for reasons to disqualify you. Don't give any to them. In addition, as the saying goes, if you act enthusiastic, you'll be enthusiastic. The reverse is also true. If you act bored, you'll be bored. . .and boring.

Don't Read

For every ten feet of linear space, you have just two to three seconds to impress an attendee enough to get him to stop. It's not impressive to see someone reading a newspaper or magazine. Save it for later.

Don't Smoke

Not only is it impolite to smoke in your booth, but it can actually offend a prospective customer; it's okay, however, to keep ashtrays in the booth for attendee use. If you really need that cigarette, schedule breaks to go somewhere else to smoke.

Don't Eat or Drink in the Exhibit

It's just plain rude and messy. Potential customers won't bother you while you're eating; they're too polite. And, of course, there are lots of other exhibits where people are waiting to sell. They don't need to talk to you.

Don't Chew Gum

No one wants to talk with someone who's chomping away at a piece of gum. Plus, trade shows are noisy. You need to be able to speak clearly and, sometimes, loudly. You can't communicate well with something in your mouth. For the same reason, avoid breath mints or Lifesavers. It's a good idea to have some breath spray or drops handy, but avoid anything that takes up space in your mouth for any length of time.

Don't Ignore Prospects

One of the rudest things you can do is ignore a prospect—even a few seconds. Nobody likes to be ignored. If you're busy when someone approaches, either acknowledge him or try to include him in your conversation. If you're talking to a boothmate or neighbor, break it off immediately.

Don't Talk on the Telephone

Why do you need a phone in your booth anyway? Every minute you spend on the phone is one less minute you could be talking to prospects, and like other trade show don'ts, it's rude. Even if the show is slow, it only takes one good prospect to make it successful. If you're on the phone, you may miss that person.

Don't Be a Border Guard

Although you want to stand close to the aisle to acknowledge attendees walking by, don't stand where you become a barricade or block the view. Stand near the aisle and off to the side, especially if you're in a ten-foot booth. (See Figure 7–1.)

Figure 7–1 Where to Stand in Your Booth

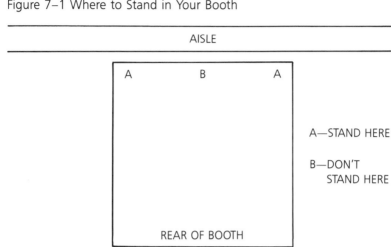

Don't Hand Out Literature to Everyone

If you've ever walked through Manhattan, you've probably had the honor of being accosted by some not-so-great-looking person holding a pile of flyers, who, as you approach, thrusts one practically into your face. Even if the literature is potentially interesting, this bold approach is offensive. So, you walk quickly away, looking for the nearest trash can. Some people don't even wait to find one—they just drop the handout on the ground. When you think about it, it's not so very different from those people at trade shows who stand in the aisle in front of their booths and thrust pieces of literature at unsuspecting attendees. Do you really want prospective customers to see you in that light?

Furthermore it's expensive, so if you don't mind, here's a money saving tip. Take only one-fourth as many pieces of literature as you originally planned. Give them all out on the first day of the show. At the end of the day, just walk around the corner to the nearest trash can, empty it out, and collect your literature. Voila! Now you've got the next day's inventory for distributing. At the end of each day, repeat this procedure. Sarcasm aside, it's just not necessary to give literature to anybody at the show, even if they ask for it. Some specific reasons follow:

Expense. The cost of printing brochures and flyers is astronomical. Look at each brochure as money. Do you really want to pass out money to anybody who asks for it? Of course not. When you just arbitrarily give away your literature, you can bet most of it will end up in the circular file. The cost of shipping literature is astronomical. Shippers charge you by weight and paper is heavy. Therefore, shipping is very expensive. Save your money.

No attendee interest. You don't want your expensive literature lost in the crowd. If the show is large, attendees may collect hundreds of pieces of literature. To avoid taking it back on the airplane, they'll cull through it at the hotel, spending about 1.3 seconds on each brochure, selecting the ones that interest them the most (about seven flyers) and tossing the other 153 four-color catalogs in the trash. Even if the show is small, it's still not practical to give out literature. No buyer wants to lug around a few pounds of unnecessary paper.

Sending literature later is good business. So how do you get valuable information to a hot prospect? Send it. Tell the prospect that you don't want to weigh her down with more literature, that you will send the requested information after the show. By doing so, you accomplish the following objectives:

First, you show how professional you are. By saying you're going to do something and then doing it, you show you are dependable. And, as Humphrey Bogart would tell you, "that's the beginning of a beautiful relationship." Second, you can personalize the follow-up with a letter. Mention some specific needs she brought out in your discussion; talk about something personal you remember from the show. Was she wearing a really sharp scarf? Did she mention playing golf? Referring to such things establishes a positive rapport. Last, it gives you a good reason to follow up by telephone. This technique creates a sense of obligation on the prospect's part to take your call. It's much easier to confirm that she received the requested material than to call out of the blue and say you met at the show. Calling then gives you an open door for moving forward in the selling process. If you just arbitrarily give out literature, you're taking a big chance. If you call, she may or may not remember you, and she may or may not still have your literature.

Don't Talk with Other Booth Personnel

I can't repeat this enough. If you give attendees a reason not to stop by your exhibit, they won't. If you look like you're busy having a conversation with someone else, they won't bother you. Keep your conversation with your boothmates and neighboring exhibit staff to the bare minimum. Talk to your potential prospects, not buddies.

Don't Underestimate Prospects

I affectionately call this the *Edith Goldman Syndrome*. I believe Edith started the trend of women wearing athletic shoes for the walk to work. Edith has been doing this for years at trade shows. One day, after attending a few hundred trade shows around the world as a buyer, she finally got fed up with aching, tired feet. So she began to wear athletic shoes. Edith didn't care what she looked like. She just wanted to be comfortable. But not all exhibitors accepted Edith with open arms. She didn't look like a buyer. But Edith is a buyer, a big buyer, one of the head buyers for Leavitt Advertising/Hanover House Industries, one of the largest mail order catalog houses in the world. They have over twenty different catalogs, including Adam York, Synchronics, and Tapestry. She was also instrumental in the start-up of one of TV's shopping channels.

Edith has the authority to buy for any part of Leavitt, which gives her considerable buying influence. But, because she wears running shoes to trade shows, not everyone takes her seriously. But Edith is philosophical about it. "If they don't take me seriously, that's their loss, not mine." And she's right.

The only people who have to look good at the trade show are the exhibit staffers. Buyers can be as comfortable as they want—blue jeans, sports shirts, slacks, whatever. Don't underestimate them.

Don't Cluster

The subliminal aspects of trade shows cannot be over-emphasized. If you get into a group discussion with two or more boothmates or other nonprospects, you're clustering. In the eyes of an attendee, you look like a corner street gang. He or she will steer clear of you, because it's very intimidating to approach a group of strangers. Create a warm, open, inviting atmosphere in your exhibit.

Be Enthusiastic

Platitudes about enthusiasm are widespread, but there's a reason for that. Enthusiasm works and it's contagious. It's not necessary to jump up and down to be enthusiastic; in fact, enthusiasm can be defined as an activity in which a lively and absorbing interest is shown. Be enthusiastic about the show and its potential. Don't let others bring you down with negative attitudes. A truly successful person doesn't look at any project without enthusiasm.

Be enthusiastic about your company and its products. To the attendee, you are your company; however you look, act, and talk will have a major influence on how the attendee perceives your company. Besides, if you're not enthusiastic about your company and its products, how can you possibly expect anybody else to be?

Be enthusiastic about yourself. One person can make a difference.

There's a story about a young girl named Annie who was institutionalized at the age of ten because she couldn't communicate, couldn't learn, and was violent. The doctors convinced her parents that Annie was hopeless. Because Annie was such a problem case, she wasn't allowed around other patients. In fact, they locked her in her room and basically threw away the key.

One nurse, however, wanted to reach Annie. So, she took her lunch breaks outside Annie's room. Each day she brought a cookie to share with Annie, which she would leave inside Annie's door. Annie cowered in fear in a corner while the nurse ate lunch just outside. Later the nurse would come back to Annie's room to clean up the smashed cookie crumbs.

One day the nurse came back to clean up the crumbs, but they were nowhere to be found. The cookie was gone and the nurse knew Annie had eaten it. Now, every day when the nurse left the cookie, Annie would eat it.

As the weeks passed, Annie slowly showed more changes. She stopped cowering in the corner. She came out to sit by the door while the nurse ate. Then one day, while the nurse was having lunch, Annie reached out, took the cookie and ate it. The nurse then knew that Annie could be educated.

Over the next few years, Annie learned to communicate with the world and became the institution's brightest student. On her eighteenth birthday, they told her she was free to leave and go on her own. But Annie didn't want to leave. She told the doctors that she wanted to stay and help others with severe learning disabilities. Annie joined the staff. Soon after, a call came to the institution. A young girl needed help. She couldn't communicate, couldn't learn, and was prone to violence. Could they send someone to work with her? With that, Annie Sullivan went to begin her work with little Helen Keller.

The point of this true story, apart from being very inspirational, is that one person can make a difference. If you are sincerely interested in helping your clients, if you truly want to solve their problems, if you have the internal enthusiasm needed to instill their confidence in you, then you will be successful beyond your wildest dreams.

Be Carefully Groomed

Wear a suit, not a sportcoat and tie. Wear ironed, starched, white shirts. Wear good ties or scarves. Get your hair cut just before you leave for the show. Make sure you have a close shave in the morning. Don't wear anything that will detract from the exhibit. Wear blues and grays; they denote professionalism, confidence, and power. Other colors turn people off. Wear black socks (men), or nude panty hose (women). Get your shoes shined every morning. If there isn't a shoeshine stand at the show, shine them yourself. As a last resort, get one of those pocket shoe polishers. If you don't have one, send me your business card, and I'll send one as a gift.

Visualize in your mind what a well-dressed person looks like and dress like that. Just remember, your clothes are not making the statement at a trade show, your company's product is. Your goal should be to wear something that the attendee won't remember. You only want them to remember your product.

Use the Prospect's Name

People love to hear their own names. Make an attendee feel important by making a concerted effort to remember his name, and then use it in the conversation from time to time.

At trade shows, people always try to glance slyly at another person's name tag. What's all the secrecy about? You probably don't know attendees' names, so you aren't insulting them by looking at their badges. Be bold; look directly at the badge and repeat the name out loud. If you have trouble pronouncing a name, ask. Tell the attendee you want to be sure and get his or her name right because you know how important your own name is to you. Most attendees will be happy to teach you the proper pronunciation. And if it's a particularly unusual name, it might prove a great opener for you.

Know Your Competition

If there's one place you should be ready to stand up to your competition, it's at a trade show. When you talk about how your product compares with the ABC Corporation, you can bet the attendee is going to go over to the ABC booth and verify your statements.

Get as much information as you can about the competition before the show and make sure your sales staff knows all about them. Then, in addition to that information, assign one or two of your competitors exhibiting at that show to each of your sales staff. Have them go through your competitors' exhibits and get the lowdown on what's new. Try to get any information that will be helpful to your cause—pricing, product comparisons, terms, delivery, freight, and the like. Obviously, no competitor will willingly give you all that information, and if your salespeople stroll into their exhibit with your company's badges on display. . . well, you know what will happen. The way to get around this is to get everybody a second badge. Go ahead and preregister them as retailers, dealers, distributors, anything that will get your competition to open up. And then send them off. Get all the info on the first day, so you can apprise each other at that night's meeting.

Another way to get this information is to ask your customers. They'll give out a lot of helpful information. They'll even tell you what the positives and negatives are about the competition, and how you stack up.

Do I feel that telling you these schemes lacks integrity? Not really. I make this suggestion to every client and audience I have.

Besides, while you're reading this little tip so is your competition. Don't say I didn't warn you.

Keep Moving in Your Booth

This is more for your own well-being than it is a selling tip, but it will make a difference if your booth is an island. By walking from one end of the booth to the other from time to time, you'll stimulate the blood flow in your legs and feet. Of course, I'm not talking about pacing back and forth; just plan to walk across the booth and back every few minutes or so. Standing for several hours creates a lot of strain on your lower body. Your legs can cramp up and your feet will be aching for days. By exercising them periodically, you'll do yourself a big favor.

When you take a break, don't just go somewhere and sit down. Give your legs a chance to limber up. Go outside, walk around, and get some fresh air. You'll be surprised at the difference in how you'll feel at the end of the four days.

For those of you working island booths and peninsulas, you absolutely must keep moving. Your exhibit can act as a barricade to attendees. If you're on one side and an attendee approaches from the other, you might never see him/her if you don't move around. Stay out toward the perimeter and keep moving. Don't stay in one place too long—you might miss somebody completely.

Be on Time for Your Shift and Be Ready

Ideally, no one should work more than four hours a day at a trade show, but for some of us it's just not possible to have more than one shift. Many companies can only afford to send one or two people to a show and they must be in the booth at all times. In these cases, being on time means being ready when the show opens.

Even on a small budget, you can still project an image of professionalism to prospects and customers. Too often I've seen companies arrive at a show to exhibit but not be ready when the doors open. This happens not only on the first day, but every other day, too. For some reason, people seem to think that it doesn't matter if attendees see them still unpacking products stored overnight. It does. Every action you make in front of a prospective customer sends a message. Do you really want to project an image of someone who's always late or whose booth is messy with boxes not yet put away? What type of message do you suppose attendees receive when they see such things?

If your exhibit is all ready to go, get to the show at least fifteen minutes before it opens. Put away your briefcase and coat and make sure the booth is clean. If you've stored product overnight, then be there at least thirty minutes early to prepare. Use any extra time to prepare yourself mentally for the coming day. If you're working all day on your feet, you'll need to program yourself mentally to have a good, positive attitude for the next eight hours.

If your company can afford to bring enough people to work shifts, then make sure the staff shows up at least fifteen minutes before their shift begins. A good idea is to overlap the shifts. If, for example, a show has hours of 10:00 A.M. to 6:00 P.M., you might run shifts like this:

9:30 A.M.–12:00 M.	Silver Team
11:45 A.M.– 2:00 P.M.	Gold Team
1:45 P.M.– 4:00 P.M.	Silver Team
3:45 P.M.– 6:30 P.M.	Gold Team

This type of schedule allows enough time in the morning to set up before the doors open, a fifteen-minute overlap for shift change, and some extra time at the end of the day to store for overnight and clean up. Although it may be a little crowded during changeover, it's a lot better to have too many salespeople than to have too few.

Be firm about the schedule. Demand that your people be on time and don't put up with laggards. A trade show is no place for someone who isn't going to support your system. I've known sales managers who actually sent salespeople home early rather than allow them to become a bad influence on the rest of the staff.

Get a Good Night's Sleep

It's common for salespeople to get together at night when they're out of town to have a little fun. There's no harm in that, but staying up late has no place at a trade show. A trade show is hard, hard work. And it's extremely hard on the body—the feet, the legs, the lower back, the eyes, and the voice. You need to give your body a chance to recuperate before the next day's onslaught. Don't go out partying until the wee hours; you'll pay for it the next day. You can't risk losing a new customer because you aren't mentally sharp enough.

Make a concerted effort to plan rest time into your trade show calendar. Give yourself time to go back to your room and unwind before going to bed. Take a Jacuzzi or short walk to loosen up. Bring a good bedtime book to read, and I don't mean a business book. Give the right side of your brain a chance to calm down from the overload it went through during the day. And then get a good night's sleep. You'll feel a lot better the next day.

There's a bit of an ego bonus, too. When you arrive at the show as fresh as a daisy, you'll be able to needle all the other salespeople who show up with hangovers. Come to think of it, you'll probably be able to outsell them, too. Hmmmm. What an interesting idea.

Don't Drink Alcohol Anytime during the Trade Show Week

Alcohol is a depressant that slows down the physical and mental processes. Alcohol causes your brain to go into slow motion. Your lips stop working, even though your mouth might not. You might accidentally slip and let out confidential information. You might embarrass yourself in front of a customer or your boss. You could wake the next morning with a hangover and be a total waste at the show. Worse still, you might not be able to work the show. It's already been established that trade shows are hard work; don't do anything that will limit your potential for success.

If you're out with a customer or prospect, drink soft drinks, or, better still, lots of water. Trade shows dehydrate the body, so drinking water replenishes your natural fluids. And the kicker is that, like getting a good night's sleep, you'll feel better when you don't drink. You'll also have an edge on those salespeople who spent the night out swapping war stories at a bar.

Don't Eat Strange or Exotic Foods

When you travel out of town to a trade show, you don't have any choice but to eat out. Do your body a favor and stick to boring, nongreasy foods. You're only asking for trouble when you try something new and different at an exotic new restaurant or local favorite. If you're not used to eating dim sum, Cajun meat loaf, or Buffalo wings, then don't try them. Your body has a hard enough time when traveling, without stuffing it with a lot of foreign substances.

Appoint One Person to Work with the Media

There's always a chance that the media might come by your booth for a story. They may be following up a lead your own company sent to them, or they may have heard about some new development or unusual products your company has introduced at the show. They may even have just strolled by and randomly selected your exhibit as one to cover for the 11:00 News. In any case, make sure you have one person assigned as the media's liaison with your company. That way you guarantee that the same story is being told at all times. If you allow anyone in your exhibit to talk with the press, you're asking for trouble. No matter how effectively you train your staff, the stories will never come out the same. In addition, the media appreciate having a special contact within the company. They know this person has been assigned to work with them, and they know they can contact this same person for a possible follow-up. The person assigned should know exactly what information is available to the media and what is not, and then stick to those guidelines.

Here are some media interview tips offered by Marilyn Hawkins, a principal in Hawkins Vander Houwen, a Seattle-based marketing and management communications agency:

- Listen as much as you talk. Understand what the reporter is asking you.
- Be friendly and engaging, but neither deferential nor defensive.
- Make your key points as simply—and as often—as possible.
- Don't ramble. Make your point and stop.
- If necessary, take time and educate the reporter. But don't do it condescendingly.
- Be quotable. Think in terms of attention-getting headlines and lead paragraphs.
- Never lie or intentionally mislead.

- Don't say anything off the record, unless you possess incredible media savvy.
- Avoid defaming anyone or anything. If the interview is about someone in particular, don't get sidetracked into talking about other people and other issues, especially negatively.
- If you don't understand the reporter's question, don't try to answer it. Politely ask for clarification.
- Never give a reporter words with which to hang yourself: "I am not a crook." "I am not a bimbo." "Go ahead and follow me, you'll be bored."
- If you don't know the answer to a question, admit it. Offer to get the answer as soon as possible, and then be sure and follow up.
- Avoid at all costs the words "No comment." There are a million ways to address a tough question short of raising that red flag.
- At the conclusion of the interview, ask the reporter if he or she got everything he or she needed.
- If the story turns out well, send the reporter a brief note of acknowledgment.

Wear Your Badge on the Right

Most people are right-handed, so they automatically put their name tag on the left side of their coat or blouse. At a show, you don't want to make it difficult for an attendee to read your name, but when you wear it on the left side, that's exactly what you're doing. The place to wear it is on the right side, near the face. The reason for this practice is that hands are shaken with the right hand. Consequently, the right shoulder leans toward the person and the left moves away. A badge worn on the right side moves toward the person being met. In addition, wearing it high makes it even easier for the attendee to read.

Keep Your Exhibit Clean

There are three things that an attendee observes immediately in every exhibit: the overall display, the personnel, and the booth's appearance. Even though you might have a service that cleans at night or comes by periodically during the day, your booth can still get cluttered and dirty. Make it a habit to inspect your booth on an ongoing basis. Empty ashtrays and trash cans; clear the area of unnecessary loose literature and other print materials; put briefcases and coats out of sight; and pick up cups and trash left behind by attendees. You might want to assign a new person during each shift to keep the booth clean. That way everybody will participate in an important, but seemingly demeaning, activity.

I know I keep harping on a lot of little things to pay attention to during the show, but it's the little things that make the difference between success and failure. There's a wise saying: "Winners make a habit of doing the things that losers don't like to do."

When You're Awake, You're Working

One of the biggest myths about trade shows is that they are some sort of vacation. Trade shows, no matter where they are, are not vacations. When done correctly, they are hard work. The hours can be long. You stand on your feet all day. You meet hundreds, possibly thousands, of strangers, taking you out of your comfort zone. You eat poorly and irregularly; convention food services have never been known for their gourmet cuisine. You get headaches from working your brain overtime. Your eyes burn from the lighting, not to mention the smoke in the arena. Your hand throbs from shaking other hands all day long. You're burned out from giving the same sales pitch over and over. You lose patience with the lookie-loos who just take up your time asking stupid questions, not to mention the kids under eighteen who snuck in past the guards.

Trade shows are not a reward, but they can be rewarding. You can take away enough business to last you several months, maybe several years. The catch is that, at a trade show, when you're awake, you're working. There are no working hours during the week of a trade show. It's not a 10 A.M. to 6 P.M. job, after which you go out with your buddies for dinner and drinks. You have to take advantage of every opportunity to contact your customers and potential prospects. Meet somebody for breakfast. Offer someone a ride to the show in your rental car, or, if you don't have one, share a taxi. At least sit next to a buyer on the bus.

When you take a break at the show, the break isn't from working, it's from standing. Take a prospect away with you for a cup of coffee. Schedule lunch with a member of the media. Arrange to meet a new customer for drinks after the show closes. And, of course, schedule dinner with someone important. Your rest period comes after dinner, in your room.

If this concept turns you off to trade shows, don't let it. It's usually only for a few days. For the amount of potential new business, you can sacrifice yourself for a few days!

Have a Hospitality Suite (Maybe)

There can only be one of two reasons to have a hospitality suite at a trade show. First, to intentionally extend the hours of the show itself. And second, to display a prototype so new, you don't want to risk your competition seeing it at the show. Hospitality suites are among the most expensive and abused of trade show costs. That's why it's important to ensure its success when having one. Here are a few points to keep in mind about hospitality suites:

Have specific objectives for the hospitality suite that are congruent with your objectives at the show. Too many companies just throw a big party. These events are too expensive and take too much planning time away from the real purpose of the trade show. Do you want to give longer and more private demonstrations of a new product to a prospect? Do you want to offer a more sedate way of displaying your products to a select few? Great! Use a hospitality suite. Do you want to impress a lot of friends, media, and enemies? Then give a party for no particular reason.

Always have a display in the suite. Why would you possibly go through the expense of having a hospitality suite, food, and refreshments without also having your product on display? Unfortunately, it happens all the time.

Set specific and reasonable hours for the suite to be open and then stick by them. The suite doesn't need to be open all night long. You'll show much more professionalism by announcing and posting that the suite is open for a specific period of time. For example, if the show ends at 6:00, have your suite open from 6:00 to 8:00 P.M.. That way you can still go out for dinner at a reasonable hour.

Make Your Restaurant Reservations Six Months Earlier

My friend Phil Wexler, coauthor of the very popular book *Non-Manipulative Selling,* passed this idea along. When you travel out of town for a show, looking for a place to eat at night gets to be a big hassle. In fact, at some of the larger shows, you might have trouble getting in to restaurants at a decent hour. Advance reservations eliminate this problem.

Phil says to make reservations as far ahead as six months before the show. Book for a decent hour, such as 7:30. Then, when you ask prospects and customers to go out at night, you look like you've got connections.

If you don't know which restaurants to call, there are several places to check. Call your hotel's concierge and ask for a list of local recommendations. *Sales and Marketing Management* magazine annually lists the top business eateries in the United States. Travel books generally list a number of good restaurants in each city. But, the best way to find where to eat is to call someone you know who lives in that city and ask him/her.

Finally, be sure to make enough reservations for your staff and any possible guests. A good rule of thumb is to double the number in your staff.

Examine the Show and Other Exhibitors

In *The Art of War,* Sun Tzu states, "What enables the good general to strike and conquer, and achieve things beyond the reach of ordinary men, is foreknowledge. Now this knowledge cannot be obtained inductively from experience, nor any deductive calculation. . . . The dispositions of the enemy are ascertainable through spies and spies alone" (77–78).

In today's business world, it's not enough to know your own product and understand the needs of your customer. You must also have complete knowledge of what the competition is doing. Trade shows are unique in that not only do the buyers come to you, but the competition is right across the aisle. It's a great opportunity for you to do some first-hand market research and information gathering. Be a spy. Take the time to walk the show thoroughly and completely.

I've already talked about having your sales staff visit the competition. Now I'll describe a little more specifically what you should be looking for while walking the show.

Look at the Show in General

As you're walking around, take in the general feel of the show. Does it seem to be a fairly upbeat atmosphere? Are the exhibitors in a good mood? Are the displays new or refurbished? Are companies spending money on this particular show? How's the attendance? If the show is sponsored by an association, talk with some of the officials. Do they feel the industry is on the upswing or is the show a downer? Are the aisles empty? Do you hear such things over the P.A. system as, "Buyer in Aisle 3,000! Buyer in Aisle 3,000," followed by exhibitors running to grab the guy?

Look for new ideas for exhibit design. What booth are you attracted to and why? What new ideas do you see that you might be able to use in future shows? What are the most crowded booths and what do they feature? What new trends do you see in these exhibits? Why are certain booths more crowded than others? Is it because they have *Playboy* centerfolds signing autographs or do they have a legitimate business reason for all the activity?

Assess the Differences between Your Company and the Competition

Part of the reason you're at the trade show is to learn as much about your competition as possible. Go ahead and be bold in approaching them. There's no law against walking into their booths and looking over their products and literature.

It's not unusual for a contingent of people to act as if they own the show. They act like the whole place is their oyster and all the information in the hall is theirs for the taking. And speaking of taking, they take pictures everywhere and of everything. Once in a while someone will walk up and ask them to stop, but not usually.

If you act like you own the place, you can get away with a lot. Get a camera and a blank note pad and go out and gather as much information as you can. Investigate your competition. Look for differences between your products, your salespeople, your exhibits, your literature, your customer perceptions, and your preshow marketing tactics and their effect on performance. (This last one doesn't necessarily have to be done at the show, but should be considered when putting all this information together.)

Once you have put this information together, you'll want to evaluate the differences by asking these questions: Is the difference positive or negative? How big is the difference? What brought on this difference and when? How does the difference affect you in the eyes of the customers? How can you respond to the difference, and how can your competitors respond? If the advantage is very much in your favor, how easy would it be for the competition to eliminate it? How can you sustain the advantage? For how long? Can you continue to build on the advantage? Other than your competition, what other factors could affect the advantage?

Maybe you can't take the time to go off during the show and gather this valuable information. If that's the case, then try to get to the show early enough to walk through undisturbed. Often, this is the best time to do it anyway. The booths are devoid of people and everything is usually displayed for your uninterrupted viewing.

Maybe you don't have the time to do all this competitor analysis. Just remember, this information will not only help you with future trade shows, it will also give you a lot of valuable information for your marketing strategy. So, if at all possible, don't let this tremendous opportunity to gather information slip away. If you can't go deeply into it, at least keep some of these questions in mind while walking the show. At least get something!

Personal Trade Show Survival Kit

As part of my services, I provide a survival kit and checklist for my clients. It's not necessary to contact me for this kit, as all the contents are easy to put together. Here's what I recommend you be sure not to forget:

- Business cards (about five times as many as you think you need)
- Corporate letterhead, note pads, and envelopes
- Breath spray (not mints or gum)
- Ballpoint pens and markers
- Your date book or pocket calendar
- Dr. Scholl's footpads (trust me, your feet will definitely know the difference)
- Comfortable shoes (this is no place to break in new ones)
- Cellophane tape and paper clips
- Large nine-by-twelve envelopes and mailing labels
- Traveler's checks and credit cards for on-site payments
- Baby powder (trust me again, each morning coat your body with it, you'll feel much fresher all day)
- Extra ties and scarves
- Shoe polish
- Band-Aids
- Aspirin or aspirin-free pain reliever
- Antacids
- Sunglasses
- Pocket stapler, staples, and staple remover
- Extra panty hose

CHAPTER 8

Postshow

Back to the Routine

The party's over. After thorough planning and preparation, you went to the trade show and knocked them dead. You effectively trained your booth staff so they obtained the maximum number of qualified leads. It seems like the ideal situation. All your customers came to see you and several hundred (maybe several thousand) new prospects crowded happily into your booth. Everyone waxed enthusiastically, you compiled lots of leads, and everyone returned home exhausted, convinced it was a good show.

Now what? Do you go back to the office and tear into that pile of mail and pink telephone slips? Or do you go home and take a couple of well-deserved days off? After all, you just worked your tail off for a week; don't you deserve a break? Sorry, the party's not over. Yes, you've successfully passed through phase one, the preshow planning phase. And you're patting yourself on the back for doing a great job on phase two, the show itself. But you've still got one more phase to go, postshow follow-up and evaluation.

Those leads you compiled are hot. Your company name is fresh in the prospect's mind. Now is the time for action, not delay.

Normally when people return from exhibiting at a trade show, they're eager to get back into the regular office routine. That's a big mistake. Don't wait to pursue all those leads from the show.

A Typical Postshow Scenario

John Smith returns after working last week's MegaTron Show in Las Vegas. He's exhausted, but knows there is a pile of old mail to open and dozens of phone calls that need to be returned. He dives into the mail and enthusiastically begins sorting it. A co-worker stops by his office asking how the show went.

"Fantastic," says John. "We worked our tails off, but it was worth it. We must have walked out with more than 600 new leads!" He then relates a couple of war stories, after which the co-worker leaves and John gets back to his mail and phone messages.

This routine continues for a day or two, when John finds out he needs to get going on a new sales campaign. Also, the new 1989 product catalog is late for production. Several strategy planning meetings with upper management require attendance, too. There's also the business trip to Region Three for the formal presentation to that big distributor. Hmmm; that nagging feeling that he has forgotten something keeps bugging John, but as the days turn into weeks, the feeling goes away.

Sound familiar? Okay, so I wrote it especially to fit the needs of this book. That's literary license. The point is, I'll bet it closely reflects most situations. What's missing from John's work? The follow-up on those 600 leads! Leads from a trade show are hot, and every day that goes by cools them down a degree or two.

I have an ongoing, informal, very unscientific survey. I make it a habit to ask trade show attendees their impressions of a recent show. I also ask how follow-up has been with them. These are *buyers* I'm talking to. The results over the last few years have been disappointing, if not downright ridiculous. For example, at the time of this writing, it is about five weeks after the Fall Comdex. This is a big show—more than 1,700 exhibitors take up 750,000 square feet, with more than 80,000 attendees. People take this show very seriously. But apparently the exhibitors don't take it seriously enough. I've already spoken with three attendees from Comdex, three legitimate buyers of high-tech products. They estimated that between them they stopped and requested information from more than 300 companies. But as of today, they have received only four follow-up responses from the show. That's less than a 2-percent response after five weeks!

Something's very wrong here. In fact, the question each of these buyers ask me is this, "If those exhibitors aren't going to bother to follow up in a timely fashion after the show, then why should I even go at all?" I have to agree.

Trade show follow-up is the reason you exhibited in the first place. Getting new leads is one of the primary objectives for attending a show. It only makes sense that those leads are of primary importance after the show is over.

The Steve Miller School of Follow-Up

Effective Follow-Up Begins before the Show Opens

This planning is very simple, easy to do, and will save you a tremendous amount of time after the show. As part of your preshow planning process, write your follow-up letter before you leave. Plug it into your word processor, leaving space for the prospect's name and address, plus room for a personalized comment. If you fill out your lead form completely, you'll have information for this section. By including one sentence that refers back to something you talked about at the trade show, the prospect won't care that he's getting a form letter. Once you get back from the show, you can give the leads to your secretary, or whoever is handling the word processor, for execution.

The Forty-Eight-Hour Follow-Up Rule

There seem to be two prevailing schools of thought regarding the time frame for follow-up. We've already discussed what I call the Infinity School of Follow-Up. That's the one where there is no time limit. You can follow up anytime. The second school of thought regarding follow-up is a fairly new one. It's the "Let's Spend Lots and Lots of Money and Get the Information to the Prospect before She Even Flies Back to Her Office — Won't She Be Impressed" School. Under this system, you send your leads at the end of each day back to the office by overnight express, where they are turned into product information kits with form letters and, in turn, sent out to the prospect by overnight express. (I hope you have a big budget.)

I've got to admit, though, if I had to pick between the Infinity School and the LSLALOMAGTITTPBSEFBTHO—WSBI School, I'd pick the second one. But it's still not good enough. On the surface it seems like a great idea, but there is a basic flaw regarding human nature that's being overlooked. After you've been out of your office for several days, what are the two things guaranteed to be waiting for you on your desk when you return? You guessed it—a two-foot stack of mail, and a one-foot stack of pink telephone messages. The average person just doesn't want to deal with these piles any longer than is absolutely necessary. As a result, she will literally buzz through them, culling out the necessary from the unnecessary just to remove the desktop clutter. She just isn't going to spend very much time on each piece of mail in her stack, even if it is a red, white, and blue express package. The process of culling through her mail will be quick. She'll spend only a few seconds on each piece, if that much.

Frankly, I don't want my expensive follow-up package to be in that pile. That's why I developed what I call the Forty-Eight-Hour Rule. The Forty-Eight-Hour Rule is simple by design, and, in my opinion, an effective way of reaching the prospect in a timely fashion. The goal of the rule is for my follow-up package to arrive no earlier than forty-eight hours after the show ends, and no later than forty-eight hours after that. Think of it as a forty-eight-hour "window." (*Note:* The Forty-Eight-Hour Rule is based on working days; it does not include weekends or holidays.)

There are four reasons for following this plan:

Visibility. You don't land in the big pile of mail. As I was just discussing, people spend about two days going through their mail and phone messages. Send your material so it lands on their desks after the big pile has been cleared off.

Memory. The show is still fresh in the prospect's mind. It's still only been a couple of days since she was at the show. If you developed a good rapport with her, she'll remember you and your product line.

Image. You told the prospect you'd be sending the information out right away, and by following this rule, you've done it. You've anchored in the prospect's mind just how professional and dependable you are.

Personal access. It gives you a reason for a follow-up telephone call. By getting the information out in such a timely manner, you can now call the prospect to check and see if she received the information.

The 5/10/20/40 Follow-Up

Once you've sent the information off to arrive within the forty-eight-hour window, you can personally follow up by telephone in a timely fashion. Unless you've already set up a personal appointment, this is the next best thing to being there.

Five working days after the show closes, your packet of information should be in the hands of the prospect. Give him a call and ask if he received the information he requested. Be sure and emphasize that you had promised to send it to him, and you are following up to make sure he received it.

If he has received the material, politely ask if he's had a chance to look through it. If he has received it and he has looked through it, then ask if you could set a phone appointment with him to discuss how you might be able to work together. Don't assume that because you've got him on the line, he has time to talk with you right then. Be considerate and offer to speak with him at his convenience. If he has received the information, but hasn't looked it over yet, then confidently say that you'll follow up in a week to answer any questions he has. This will put the onus on him to look through the packet. If he hasn't received the information yet, simply say you're sure he'll receive it in a day or two and you'll follow up again next week. Again, make sure to set the phone appointment.

The object of the 5/10/20/40 Follow-Up is that you talk with the prospect five working days after the show, and then ten, twenty, and forty working days after the show. By the fortieth day, you should know where you stand with him. This is not to say that you must talk with him all four times. If you close the deal on the second call, then you don't need to continue this pattern. Of course, good customer service after the sale is important, but that's another issue.

The beauty of the 5/10/20/40 Follow-Up is that in a short period of time, you know exactly where you stand. If that prospect has a need and a desire, you know you'll be staying on top of that person until you get the order. If, for whatever reason, you determine that he doesn't fit your criteria for a prospect, then you can stop spending your valuable time on him.

One additional objective I have in that time frame is to get the name of another possible contact from the prospect. After meeting him at the show and following up regularly, I usually build a fairly good rapport with the prospect. Because of this good rapport, I can ask for referrals, whether or not we do business together. In fact, sometimes the ones I don't work with feel a sense of obligation to help me because of the time I've put into building our relationship.

Remember, the three parts of the trade show campaign are before, during, and after the show. Your goal is to use preshow marketing effectively to entice customers and prospects to visit your booth at the trade show. Then, through professional trade show selling and presenting, you bring yourself one step closer to your goals. Then, with timely and effective postshow follow-up, you tie the three parts together synergistically. You have taken what was in the past a two-, three-, four-, or five-day event, and turned it into a very successful four- to five-month marketing campaign.

The Evaluation

Evaluation is what most people consider to be the hardest part of trade show marketing. Actually, if you set those measurable objectives in the beginning that I discussed in Chapter 2, this is the easy part.

There is another way, however, that will help you measure the success of your trade shows easily and effectively. Essentially it is a three-step process, requiring that you set quantitative goals to be measured at three different time intervals: immediately following the show, six months later, and again twelve months later. With this method, all you need to do is compare the results of your show with the original objectives.

Let's say, for example, your three objectives are:

Immediate—500 leads
6 months—20 new accounts
12 months—20 additional new accounts

What this means is that you expect to leave the show with 500 solid leads. Then, within the next six months, you expect to turn them into twenty new accounts, and after an additional six months, you expect to acquire twenty more new accounts, directly attributable to the show.

This process is fairly simple, requiring only a customer profile form that includes information on where the lead came from. You should have that anyway. It's important you know whether your new customers come from a direct mail campaign, customer referrals, cold calls, or trade shows. Such information gives you a direction on where to focus your marketing efforts.

Some of your goals may be more difficult to measure, but you should still do your best. For example, let's say you want to create a new corporate image through an updated logo. Your exhibit is designed to focus on your new look, so your objective is to have as many people come through your booth as possible. You still want their business cards, but don't have the staff size to qualify everybody. Offer some sort of dynamite incentive to get them to leave their business cards, such as a drawing for an all-expense-paid trip to Hawaii. By totaling the number of business cards you receive, you'll know how many people came through your booth. This would equal the number of impressions your new logo made. Then, after the show, do a follow-up telemarketing campaign to accomplish two things. First, to determine the impact your new logo made, and second, to qualify potential prospects. This way, you're not only measuring a nebulous goal, but getting some solid leads, as well.

While your objectives for a show may not be one of these, it is important that you do have some objectives on paper for postshow evaluation. Too many companies never evaluate their trade shows and that's a mistake. Just like any other strategy in your marketing mix, you need to measure the success or failure of each risk.

The Decision to Return

Most companies automatically sign up for a show after it appears that the show was worthwhile. Considering that most companies don't even measure the success or failure of a show, other than by gut feeling, this can be a real mistake.

Every time you consider going to a show, even if you've been going for years, you must make sure that show is right for you. Companies change, trends change, industries change, markets change, and trade shows change. When you consider returning to a show, reread Chapter 2 and use the listed guidelines for selecting a show. Then go to four other sources for more feedback.

Customers

Ask them whether they believe the show is still one your company should attend. They'll be straight with you. Something may have changed in the show over the years so your customers no longer feel that the show has value for you.

Staff

These people work the show floor. They should know whether or not the show still works for your company.

Competition

Your competition is a valuable source of information. If the trade show is moving away from your original objectives, it's probably moving away from those of your competitors, too. If you've got a good relationship with them, ask their opinion.

Trade Journals

Trade journals know what's happening in the industry. If a trade show is in trouble, or is changing markets, the journals should know about it. They can give you their opinion on exhibiting in the show.

Trade shows are expensive and time consuming. Don't just arbitrarily make a decision to go to a show because you think it's right. Be ruthless in your determination to make an intelligent decision. After all, it's your money and your time.

A Look Ahead

Although the trade show industry is very large, with estimates placed as high as $50 billion spent annually on exhibitions, I believe we are only in the infancy stage. Innovations for more effective shows are developed every day. Exhibitors are becoming more sophisticated in their techniques and more demanding of their results.

I've stressed the importance of the Q.I.S.S. principle at trade shows. Qualifying Is Smart Selling. This may be the most critical factor at any trade show.

One innovation I feel compelled to write about is from Free World Marketing, of Newport Beach, California. They've developed a new system for registering attendees at shows. The first stage in registration has been the plain, old, paper badge, imprinted with name, company, and city. The last few years have brought a proliferation of the credit-card type badge, the second stage, enabling exhibitors to use a standard credit card imprinter for recording an attendee's name, address, and phone number. Although this was supposed to help speed up the process of generating leads, it did very little to help qualify them. Enter the third stage. Free World has developed a new software lead tracking program designed with trade show managers and exhibitors in mind. The program is called ProMotion.

For the most part, ProMotion does what a lot of other sales lead management software does. It integrates your data base of contacts with your word processor, lets you create a letter library, dials your telephone, reminds you of phone appointments, tracks calls made, prints correspondence and mailing labels, and lets you search on defined fields. What separates ProMotion from other software and why it's so great for trade shows is its ability to read magnetic stripes. Now a registration badge can contain an attendee's name, address, and phone number as well as information on product interests, purchasing authority, buying time frame, and other important qualifying features. By having a magnetic reader and a computer in your booth, you can now learn about your prospect while you're standing there talking to him! The ability to qualify instantly gets nearer and nearer.

Another new trend that's picking up steam is the private trade show. Companies are finding out it's possible to hold their own personal show and have private audiences with their top prospects. If your company is diversified enough and big enough, you might be able to justify such a venture.

A couple of other trends to keep an eye out for are in the communications field. More and more companies will use cellular telephones and fax machines at trade shows. Obviously the cellular phones will be easier to use because of their portability. The fax machines will be used to send leads back to the office for follow-up. It might go against my Forty-Eight-Hour Rule, but it's still going to be a big hit.

New trends and developments in computers, audio-visual presentations, sales techniques, communications, and lead tracking will certainly make trade shows more efficient and effective. They will also enhance the value of trade shows, making them more and more important.

Don't get lost in the crowd by staying in the same old rut of trade show participation. Use the methods and techniques described in this book, and then be on the outlook for other new tools you can use. This is not the final chapter of this book. There will always be more information to share with you.

Where to Get More Information

Here are a number of different sources you may want to contact for further information:

Exhibit Designers and Producers Association
611 E. Wells Street
Milwaukee, WI 53202
414/276-3372

Exhibit Surveys
Box 327
Middletown, NJ 07748
201/741-3170

Exposition Service Contractors Association
400 S. Houston Street
Union Square
Dallas, TX 75202
214/744-9902

Health Care Exhibitors Association
5775 Peachtree-Dunwoody Road
Suite 500-D
Atlanta, GA 30342
404/252-3663

International Association of Convention and Visitors Bureaus
P.O. Box 758
Champaign, IL 61820
217/359-8881

International Exhibitors Association
5103-B Backlick Road
Annandale, VA 22003
703/941-3725

National Association of Exposition Managers
719 Indiana Avenue
Suite 300
Indianapolis, IN 46202-3135
317/638-6236

Trade Show Bureau
1660 Lincoln Street
Suite 2080
Denver, CO 80264
303/860-7626

Publications

Exhibitor
745 Marquette Bank Building
Rochester, MN 55903
507/289-6556

Exhibit Builder
P.O. Box 4144
Woodland Hills, CA 91365
800/356-4451

Successful Meetings
633 Third Avenue
New York, NY 10017
212/986-4800

Tradeshow and Convention Guide
49 Music Square West
Nashville, TN 37203
615/321-4250

"Tradeshow & Exhibit Manager"
Goldstein & Associates
1150 Yale Street
Suite 12
Santa Monica, CA 90403
213/828-1309

Tradeshow Week Publications
12233 W. Olympic Boulevard
Suite 236
Los Angeles, CA 90064
213/826-5696

Index

About the Author

Steve Miller is an independent trade show marketing consultant based in Seattle. He has eleven years of international trade show marketing experience working with and consulting for associations, show management companies, foreign companies, and corporate America, including several *Fortune* 500 companies.

Steve grew up with myasthenia gravis, a supposedly incurable form of muscular dystrophy, but defeated the disease and went on to lead a healthy and active life, including a short stint on the PGA golf tour. He now lives in Seattle with his best friend Kay—his wife.

As a speaker and trainer, Steve's programs on trade show marketing and selling have received high acclaim. His company, The Adventure, offers seminars, keynote speeches, and consulting, as well as audio and video programs. He is also a member of the National Speakers Association.

For more information, call or write:

The Adventure
33422 30th Avenue S.W.
Federal Way, WA 98023
206/874-9665
FAX 206/874-9666

TITLES OF INTEREST IN
MARKETING AND SALES PROMOTION
FROM NTC BUSINESS BOOKS

Contact: 4255 West Touhy Avenue
Lincolnwood, IL 60646-1975
800-323-4900 (in Illinois, 708-679-5500)

SUCCESSFUL DIRECT MARKETING METHODS, Fourth Edition, by Bob Stone

PROFITABLE DIRECT MARKETING by Jim Kobs

READINGS AND CASES IN DIRECT MARKETING by Herb Brown and Bruce Buskirk

SUCCESSFUL TELEMARKETING by Bob Stone and John Wyman

HOW TO CREATE SUCCESSFUL CATALOGS by Maxwell Sroge

BEST SALES PROMOTIONS, Sixth Edition, by William A. Robinson

INSIDE THE LEADING MAIL ORDER HOUSES, Third Edition, by Maxwell Sroge

NEW PRODUCT DEVELOPMENT by George Gruenwald

THE COMPLETE TRAVEL MARKETING HANDBOOK by Andrew Vladimir

HOW TO TURN CUSTOMER SERVICE INTO CUSTOMER SALES by Bernard Katz

THE MARKETING PLAN by Robert K. Skacel

ADVERTISING & MARKETING CHECKLISTS by Ron Kaatz

SECRETS OF SUCCESSFUL DIRECT MAIL by Richard V. Benson

U.S. DEPARTMENT OF COMMERCE GUIDE TO EXPORTING

HOW TO GET PEOPLE TO DO THINGS YOUR WAY by J. Robert Parkinson

HOW TO WRITE A SUCCESSFUL MARKETING PLAN by Roman G. Hiebing, Jr., and Scott W. Cooper

101 TIPS FOR MORE PROFITABLE CATALOGS by Maxwell Sroge

HOW TO GET THE MOST OUT OF TRADE SHOWS by Steve Miller

MARKETING TO CHINA by Xu Bai Yi

STRATEGIC MARKET PLANNING by Robert J. Hamper and L. Sue Baugh

COMMONSENSE DIRECT MARKETING, Second Edition, by Drayton Bird

NTC'S DICTIONARY OF MAILING LIST TERMINOLOGY AND TECHNIQUES by Nat G. Bodian